CABIN

ALSO BY LOU URENECK

Backcast: Fatherhood, Fly-fishing, and a River Journey
Through the Heart of Alaska

CABIN

*Two Brothers, a Dream
and Five Acres in Maine*

LOU URENECK

VIKING

VIKING
Published by the Penguin Group
Penguin Group (USA) Inc., 375 Hudson Street, New York, New York 10014, U.S.A. · Penguin
Group (Canada), 90 Eglinton Avenue East, Suite 700, Toronto, Ontario, Canada M4P 2Y3 (a
division of Pearson Penguin Canada Inc.) · Penguin Books Ltd, 80 Strand, London WC2R
0RL, England · Penguin Ireland, 25 St. Stephen's Green, Dublin 2, Ireland (a division of Penguin
Books Ltd) · Penguin Books Australia Ltd, 250 Camberwell Road, Camberwell, Victoria 3124,
Australia (a division of Pearson Australia Group Pty Ltd) · Penguin Books India Pvt Ltd, 11
Community Centre, Panchsheel Park, New Delhi – 110 017, India · Penguin Group (NZ), 67
Apollo Drive, Rosedale, Auckland 0632, New Zealand (a division of Pearson New Zealand
Ltd) · Penguin Books (South Africa) (Pty) Ltd, 24 Sturdee Avenue, Rosebank, Johannesburg
2196, South Africa

Penguin Books Ltd, Registered Offices: 80 Strand, London WC2R 0RL, England

First published in 2011 by Viking Penguin, a member of Penguin Group (USA) Inc.

10 9 8 7 6 5 4 3 2 1

ISBN 978-0-670-02294-6

Printed in the United States of America
Designed by Carla Bolte

For Paul,
there from the beginning

The sun illuminates only the eye of the man, but shines into the eye and heart of the child.

—Emerson

CONTENTS

CHAPTER 1

THE URGE TO BUILD

The idea had taken hold of me that I needed nothing so much as a cabin in the woods—four rough walls, a metal roof that would ping under the spring rain and a porch that looked down a wooded hillside.

I had been city-bound for nearly a decade, dealing with the usual knockdowns and disappointments of middle age. I had lost a job, my mother had died and I was climbing back from a divorce that had left me nearly broke. I was a little wobbly but still standing, and I was looking for something that would put me back in life's good graces. I wanted a project that would engage the better part of me, and the notion of building a cabin—a boy's dream, really—seemed a way to get a purchase on life's next turn. I won't lie. I needed it badly.

So, on a day of warm September sunshine in 2008, after having bought a piece of land in western Maine the previous February, I stood in a corner of my brother Paul's suburban backyard in Portland and examined a stack of lumber I had dropped there more than a decade earlier. I had to stomp down the weeds with my brown leather brogues to get to it. I hadn't yet bought a pair of work boots. I was dressed for the classroom, where I now earned my living, disguised as a college professor: khaki trousers, button-down cotton shirt and semiround tortoiseshell glasses. I confronted the wood; or maybe, as a symbolic artifact of an earlier life, it confronted me. It was a temporary standoff with the past. Piled chest high, the wood made an incongruous sight among the neighborhood's turquoise swimming pools, oversized gas grills and slumping badminton nets. To a passerby, it must have looked like a heap of old railroad ties dumped by the side of the road. I brushed the rough surface of the wood with my hand and pressed a thumbnail into its pulpy flesh. It was spongy: not a good sign. A few of the boards showed sawdust and smooth channels that were the work of carpenter ants. There were many more pieces— heavy posts, big square beams and long silvery rafters with bird's-mouth mortises—that had come through the years of sun and snow mostly sound. I couldn't help feeling some affinity with the wood: weathered but mostly intact. This was what I had hoped for on the drive up from Boston, where I lived and worked. I had counted on salvaging enough lumber from the pile to form the frame of the cabin that already had taken shape in my mind.

Paul stood with me in his backyard. He was less sure about the wood.

"I don't know," he said. "A lot of it's wet, maybe rotten."

Paul is an experienced and methodical builder. He typically works with architects, engineers, cranes and shipments of steel. He is the construction and project manager for a commercial real estate company in Portland—its vice president, in fact. He is a nonconformist in other parts of his life—a big man with a thick mustache, he drives a Harley-Davidson motorcycle wearing a sleeveless undershirt, open leather vest and a head kerchief tied tightly above his ears for a helmet—but he is cautious in matters of construction, the equivalent of the prudent and spectacled accountant. He applies conservative principles to the building of things, and he was exercising his professional caution on my woodpile. He might as well have been a banker sniffing weak collateral. I, on the other hand, was determined to work up the cabin from the old lumber, which would seriously reduce the project's cost and give me a rustic shelter that was an appreciation of the beauty of wood, and I wanted to get started right away. I was feeling the burden of his skepticism.

"The roof is going to have to carry a big snow load in those hills," Paul said.

I could feel him inching closer to saying what he was actually thinking, which was that I should forget the woodpile and have a fresh bundle of two-by-four studs delivered from the lumberyard. That after all was the sensible thing to do: new lumber, new windows, prehung doors and prefabricated roof trusses. We could hire some help, engage subcontractors for the plumbing and electricity and have the cabin up in a few weekends. I would summarize his attitude as "Let's make this easy and get to the part where we sit inside and enjoy the place."

Instead, I wanted to construct the cabin with these big woebegone slabs of wood in the old timber-frame method of building a barn, which meant employing, as much as possible, old-fashioned wood joinery rather than nails. It would hold together in much the same way as a chest of drawers assembled in a furniture shop. I wanted a place with some craft and heft and tradition—a place that could make a natural and authentic claim to a piece of rugged Maine hillside. I didn't want a vacation home; I wanted a cabin. The rough-sawn and weathered beams, as I planned it, would be exposed inside the cabin just as they would be in a barn or backwoods Maine camp, and it would be sturdy and raised up from local materials, and it would be all the better for requiring the expenditure of time and skill with a mallet, wood chisel and framing square. And I wanted for us to do it all ourselves.

Paul listened to all of this without passing judgment or rolling his eyes. He was keeping an open mind, but I knew that I already had raised his suspicions when I showed him a bunch of dilapidated wood-frame windows I had scrounged over the summer for the price of hauling them away. They also were stored in his backyard.

Paul slid a rafter out of the pile that had the surface texture of Roquefort cheese. It was a good sixteen feet long. Its edges were gnawed and ragged. It crumbled in his hands.

"I'm not sure I want to be standing under this one when the snow on the roof gets to be four feet deep."

I had to agree with him about that particular rafter. It was awfully ratty and might snap under a load of wet snow.

"You're right," I said, wanting to keep him engaged in the project.

In this experiment in mental health, building the cabin with Paul was one of the reasons I wanted to build it at all. When you get around to reassembling your life, as I was doing, it's good to have someone at your side who remembers how the parts once fit together.

"Let's spread the wood out on the grass and put the bad pieces in a pile," I said. "We'll see what we have left."

Paul was agreeable, which is his natural disposition. His agreeableness is broken only now and again by a surfeit of suburban life. Then he gets gruff, bossy and next to impossible. He had inherited our mother's need for a little danger to keep life interesting, and when he doesn't get it, he turns surly. At present, he was living in a five-bedroom garrison with his wife, Laura, and their blended family of eight children, six of whom were at home, one at college, and another, Paul's oldest son, on a tour of duty in Iraq. Even in the best of times, when he accommodated himself to the routines of mowing the lawn, painting window trim or putting out citronella candles for a backyard barbecue for his and the neighbors' kids, Paul's silent argument with the suburbs had a way of showing through. He was the only person in the neighborhood with a disassembled body of a stock car on blocks in the driveway.

Paul's cantankerous bouts come two or three times a year. They are usually cured by long trips on his Harley. It is a black-and-chrome monster with studded leather saddlebags. When he drops his two hundred twenty pounds down on the leather saddle and turns the key, it sounds like a 727 accelerating for takeoff at Logan Airport. The muffler blows out a bass line that reverberates in the chest cavity of anyone standing nearby. The bike is his antidote to the suburban blues. The miles on the road with the engine roaring below him, the wind in his dense curly hair and the absence of lawn sprinklers bring him back into balance and an even temperament. After a long bike trip, he returns with stoicism and equanimity to work at his real estate company's downtown office, to face yard chores at home and meetings of the church parish council, where he has become indispensable to the building committee and is the closest and perhaps only confidant of the church's serious but excitable priest. Having just come home from a bike rally week in Florida, Paul was being unusually patient with me, his older brother, the professor. He wore a black Harley T-shirt with red flames that read "Ride It Like You Stole It."

"Okay, what the hell," Paul said. "Let's pick through it and see what we've got."

We discussed each stick of lumber as if we were putting together a football team from a field of tryouts. Yes to this one, no to that one. Some pieces clearly were rejects. We picked them up together and tossed them into the discard pile. They landed with a slap and rumble. Others were solid. We restacked them in a neat pile with lathing sticks between to keep them ventilated and dry. Many pieces fell somewhere in between: possibly usable depending on what we would ask of them. These required longer conversations. A questionable timber might work as a post where the stress would be downward compression; it wouldn't work as a horizontal beam, where the rot would result in it snapping, toothpick-style. We took our time under the blue sky. It was a pleasant day for this kind of easy labor. I liked the weight and feel of the wood and the workout it was giving my arms and back, and it was roughing up my hands, which had grown used to paper and keyboards. Paul's company was a tonic. It was good to be with him again after a long absence. He had a way of anchoring me in our mutual past and keeping me steady in a reliable present.

As we went through the wood, I tried to rationalize each piece. Paul was more likely to say, "What, are you kidding? Forget it." He paused. "Are you sure you don't want to buy new lumber?"

A cabin gets built in three steps. There is the placement of the footing on which the cabin rests; there is the assembly of the simple box that is the cabin itself, and this includes the top of the box that is the roof; and finally there is the collection of final decisions and touches about the interior space that make the cabin habitable. The size and position of doors and windows fit in the second step but influence much of the third. The first step teaches all of the figurative truths associated with sure foundations and good beginnings. "Well begun is half done." This is one of many builders' homilies that apply to an awful lot of life in general. "Measure twice, cut once" is another. The real action of the cabin is the box: it defines the space and consumes most of the builder's effort and materials and displays his skill. A well-built cabin is an aesthetic as well as practical statement, and, on the high end, it is a manifesto of craft and simplicity. It blends function and beauty in the way of a Shaker chair, an Indian sweetgrass basket or even a Stillson plumber's wrench. The beauty derives from elegance of function. There is nothing extra, nothing fake. The final step of building moves the cabin from habitable to comfortable and even pleasing to the soul. So there is a hierarchy of sorts, from boots-in-the-mud foundation work to the Zen of sitting in front of a window that is exactly the right height and position to show the fall of the land toward a distant prospect on which the satisfied builder's attention is focused. Maybe this prospect is a gnomish hemlock tree silhouetted against the gray November sky, allowing the builder in repose to dissolve into the landscape and achieve his yogic samadhi.

Paul and I had been through this before—right down to the search for a mutually tolerable midpoint between my absorption in the history of vernacular New England carpentry and his intention to get the goddamned thing built.

Thirty years earlier, when we were in our twenties, we had built a house together, my first (and only) house as a married man. It was a simple, honest, mostly square and plumb cape with a redbrick chimney down the center. It had four bedrooms, one and a half baths, a big kitchen, dining room, living room and full basement. It was shingled with Canadian white cedar, four inches of each overlapping shingle showing to the weather. The shingle spacing gave it the lateral lines of a Maine planked dory without the upward sweep. It was stained silver-gray, like a weathered beach cottage, with Cabot bleaching oil. Wide pine boards formed the floors. The door and window trim were white, and it had a twelve-inch overhang on the eave and one-over-one pitch on the roof, which meant that the roof rose one vertical foot for each foot of horizontal span. In other words, the roof was steep. It was a handsome and modest house at the end of a long driveway, and with the exception of a designer window near the peak of one side wall, it looked like it had been built two hundred years ago. It sat on fifteen acres in a small farming community northwest of Portland. I had insisted on timber framing that one too, in the old and traditional way. It was as if I were doing fieldwork for a dissertation in colonial architecture and Paul was building a house for his brother.

The story of the lumber that Paul and I were sorting in his backyard on that day in September nested inside the story of that first house, and if nothing else, the one story giving birth to the other showed that I hadn't fully left my old life behind. There was something encouraging for me in the realization of the connection. If there's one thing that I had yearned for in my life, it was coherence. I just didn't seem to have the talent for it. I felt like I had been stringing together a series of isolated episodes, punctuated by failures, with one episode seeming to bear no relation to the next. This, I think, had been a source of the drizzly moods that sometimes descended on me. It's difficult to give your life meaning if you can't give it coherence.

So looking back, maybe the backyard lumber was a way for me to knit together two episodes of my life, two dreams, really, one that had cracked long ago and another that was about to commence.

Here is a sequence from the first dream:

In 1975, having been married for one year and most definitely, completely and unarguably without money, I decided to build a house. My bride wanted a house, and I wanted to give her one. I simply needed to materialize it out of optimism and thin air. I was twenty-four and working at the daily newspaper in Portland and persuaded my employee credit union to lend me $7,500 with no collateral, no credit history and only fourteen months of employment. I bought a piece of land about a forty-five-minute drive from Portland—the land got a lot cheaper as you got farther out of town. We had been renting the second-floor apartment of a wooden three-decker in a distressed part of Portland. My only asset was a willingness to work. I was at that stage of life when young confidence blends with the illusion that time and possibility are limitless—I could draw on them forever to build a career, a house, or whatever it was I thought I wanted to do. I was brash. Why not build a house? Maybe it would take a year; maybe two years. Money? No problem. I would borrow it. Tools? Easily solved. I would buy them at the hardware store as I needed them, and I would do all of this while working full-time as the assistant city editor of a small daily newspaper. But even I knew that building an entire house was not a job for one person. I needed another set of hands just to carry the other end of a long board. So I called Paul.

Paul was twenty-one, and he had just quit a factory job in New Jersey. Only months before and despite good grades, he had left Monmouth College in Long Branch, New Jersey, mostly out of disgust with the gap, as he saw it, between the need for a revolution in America and the hypocrisy of college life as embodied in the privileged attitudes of rich girls from Long Island—of which many populated Monmouth College. Paul had always harbored a very low tolerance for hypocrisy, or to use the more direct term, bullshit. He was, at the time, deeply radicalized over the war in Vietnam. His hair was kinky and long, and he had a tight-coiled beard and dense eyebrows. It would have been easy to mistake him for Che Guevara—if Che Guevara had been the son of a Slavic father. There was also this: he had recently ended an intense relationship with his college girlfriend. The breakup was painful. So close were they that it had seemed to me a tearing of flesh. She was the daughter of a wealthy family from Philadelphia. She had soft dark eyes and the same antiwar politics as Paul. Paul told me much later that he had seen those big soft brown eyes of hers only once again in his life: in a doe that had died slowly beside the road after it had been struck by a car.

Out of college, out of work and without a girlfriend, Paul was untethered and looking for the next thing in his life. He has always been one to move on—Paul is not a brooder, the opposite of me. Coherence is not a big concern of his; or rather, I should say, he possesses it naturally, and from within, and not with conscious consideration. Or, as he has counseled me through the years, "There are times when you can think about things too much." This readiness of his to move on was in 1975, and he had just bought a blue 1955 Chevy pickup truck. He was busy rebuilding the engine in an extra room of our mother's apartment in Lakewood, New Jersey, where he was living when I called him about the house I wanted to build.

"Sure," he said. "I can come up."

He finished work on the truck, drove it to Maine and moved in with my wife and me—we had a small spare bedroom in our apartment.

Neither of us had built a house all the way through before. We had the experience of summer construction jobs growing up in rural South Jersey. In college I had worked on a framing crew; Paul had worked as a Sheetrock installer. So we learned the rest of it as we went along. I bought a pile of books and studied the pine-and-oak-ribbed cavities of nineteenth-century barns scattered around the Maine countryside.

The house we built was not perfect but—being way, way overbuilt, with the intent to last forever—it most definitely captured my inner psychic complexity at the time. I wanted permanence. I fell somewhat short of the mark. My wife and I spent nearly twenty years of marriage in it, some of them happy, and together we raised our two children, Elizabeth and Adam, in it.

In the mid-nineties, as the marriage was coming unglued, we put the house up for sale. I decided, as a final act of ownership, to hire a man to clear a stand of big pine trees on a corner of the property. The trees were beauties: tall and straight as pencils but thick as carpenter's crayons. They had been pruned of their lower branches years earlier to create clear white wood—furniture-quality wood. A truck hauled the logs to a nearby sawmill, and I paid a carpenter to cut and shape the lumber into the framing members that would eventually form a set of cabins. I more or less left it to the carpenter to figure out the work based on what the trees gave up for boards and beams. I had no mental picture of what I wanted the lumber to become. "Work it out as best you can," I told him. I vaguely had in mind a set of small cabins that one day might be arranged near a pond somewhere to make a family compound, something like the Kennedys had at Hyannis Port, but on a workingman's scale. I imagined children and grand-children running and jumping into the pond off a long wooden dock, canoes tipped over in the grass and rocking chairs on the porch. I think I had seen that picture in a movie once.

Of course, none of this family-retreat fantasy fit the reality of my true situation. Aligning aspiration with reality has never been a strong point with me. This is the gene that *I* inherited from our mother, and in better times might account for whatever progress I have made in my life. In other words, I sometimes didn't know what I shouldn't attempt. But back then, as the carpenter was do-ing his work on my lumber, I was a man on an icy slope toward divorce who was simultaneously assembling the pieces of a family

retreat. I haven't yet found the right analogy to capture the con-
flicted quality of my life then: maybe a man fixing his porch on
the morning of the day he knows he will burn down his house.
Was it desperation or delusion? I don't know. But clearly I had an
obsession with shelter. The reason for claiming those trees as future
cabins would have been perfectly obvious to any slightly self-aware
person, but I was not paying a lot of attention then to my deeper
motivations. My gaze was ahead, not back or inward. I wasn't able
to see the submerged reasons until much later, when I started trying, with the help of a psychiatrist, to understand why I was coming seriously unhinged.

Stories are like hens. They hatch new stories. So here's another
story, and it stands in a row behind the stories of the woodpile
and the house we built in 1975 and even the marriage that cracked
—it's all part of a long line of explanation that leads to the cabin.

Growing up, I had always been on the move, from one place
to another, sometimes in the middle of the night. My mother and
father had separated several times when I was very young, and my
father disappeared from my life when I was seven years old. There
was no explanation from him or my mother. There was no last
day with him; he was simply not there anymore. Following his
departure, my childhood became a succession of rentals—small
homes or apartments in which we often lived for just a few months
before departing—with the rent unpaid and the security deposit
sacrificed. My mother was a beautician, and the foundation of her
income (and our lives) were her skills and hard work and a small
suitcase that contained several pairs of scissors, combs, frocks,
curling irons, a handheld hair dryer, a tin of wax, tweezers and
other tools of the hairdresser's trade. There was also a vibrator in

there, which she said was for massaging the scalp, but now that I'm older I have to wonder.

For a while she had her own shop; then she worked for others. Sometimes she did hair at home; sometimes she went to the homes of her customers. She was very good at what she did, and she enjoyed it, but still we were nearly always broke. A five-dollar tip meant we were flush: a pizza with all the toppings for dinner. She received a few dollars a month in child support from my father, but it was hardly enough to cover a week's groceries—not to mention the rent. This meant that there were times when there was no choice but to pick up and leave. Moving was no tragedy for my mother, at worst an inconvenience. I think she enjoyed the change of scenery and the drama that accompanied these moves. I once counted seventeen different places my mother, Paul and I had lived before I went off to college. All of these moves were tightly clustered in two areas: Spotswood, in central New Jersey, where I was born, and Toms River, on the Jersey shore, where I went to middle and high school.

From time to time, the memory of one of those rented houses or apartments comes back to me. It usually begins with an association like the smell of frying pork chops or the sight of a rain-smeared window. I feel a nostalgic hum when one of these sensations is pregnant with the memory of a home that slumbers hidden in my past, and if I sit with one long enough, I can usually stalk it back to its source, very often a house in which I ate, played or did my homework as a boy. I love the smell of frying pork chops, and the sight of a rain-smeared window can make me tear up. Behind the pork chop smell is an indistinct vignette of a woman my mother had hired to watch Paul and me while she was at work. The woman, our babysitter, is fat, wears an apron and stands at the stove. I look at her from behind, and the flesh at her elbows is loose like on a baby's legs. The cool autumn air comes through the kitchen window, lifts the curtain and brings me the delicious aroma of the searing pork fat as I wait for supper. I cannot account for the emotion behind the wet window—I know only that in the memory I am alone in a big house and the rain is steadily falling. I am warm and out of the weather. I don't even know if we lived there.

Sometimes I count back over the houses. Of the places we lived, the one I liked the best was a bungalow on Polonia Street in Spotswood. I was about eight. Polonia Street was less than a quarter mile from dead end to dead end and lined on both sides with small wood-framed homes on tiny lots. One end of the street faded into a patch of woods that contained a three-story house with a mansard roof occupied by two ancient women who wore long shapeless dresses and high lace-up shoes. We called it the haunted house. We would sneak up to the door, bang the big knocker and run away in fear and delight. The other end of the street went right up to the wire-and-wood fence that enclosed a horse pasture adjacent to a small ramshackle stable kept by a man who gave pony rides at fairs and amusement parks. There was something creepy yet secretly alluring about the place, mixing, as it did, teenage girls in cowboy boots and scruffy male ponies who seemed frequently tumescent in their presence. So you might say this period of my childhood was bounded on one end by danger (the haunted house) and on the other by the suggestion of depravity (the horse pasture). Home in the middle was security.

Our Polonia Street house had a kitchen, bathroom, living room and bedroom downstairs and two bedrooms upstairs—one for Paul and one for me. The upstairs bedrooms were on either side of the house with a stubby hall between them that led to a front window tucked inside a snug dormer, where there was a window seat. I remember sitting on it watching the limbs of a big tree brush the roof and listening to the sounds of the house—my mother in the kitchen downstairs, Paul in his bedroom playing with his toys, the television on in the living room. I don't remember any winter scenes from this house, which suggests we were there for less than a year's full cycle of seasons. There was a small front yard with a cement sidewalk to the front door, and a somewhat bigger backyard that went right up to the tracks of the Camden–Amboy railroad. The train clicking by at night would put me into a deep sleep.

Johnny, my mother's boyfriend, was already living with us then and a comfortable part of our lives. He did most of the housework; having been in the navy, he cleaned the house as if he were a seaman swabbing the deck of a ship. I would come home, the floors wet and the house smelling so strongly of ammonia that my eyes would burn.

It was a cozy house. It had a roomy kitchen with a deep porcelain sink, and a view over the sink to the train tracks and the huge field beyond, where men would hunt rabbits in the fall. The muffled faraway gunshots were exciting. Even now, the memory of coming in through the back door into the linoleum kitchen and encountering the small kitchen table gives me pleasure. Why this house on Polonia Street stays with me so permanently and why it is the place I can most easily see Paul and me as children is a mystery. Maybe it is because the house was comfortable, cozy and simple, and we lived there with Johnny as a family. It was a happy time, a brief period of calm.

This recollecting of houses has been a kind of reverse senescence with me: the older I get, the more I remember of the places where I lived as a child, and the more valuable the past has seemed to become. In my darker moments, when the past shimmers with more appeal than the future, I know to be on my guard—a melancholic mood is about to fall over me. It is like the premonitory aura that precedes a migraine headache. I recall some homes that Paul can't, which makes sense since I am almost four years older than he. He has recalled one or two that I have forgotten. He has always had the better memory, right down to the details of the model-airplane decals that we pasted on our knotty-pine bunk beds. He remembers that I slept on the upper bunk, he on the bottom. But I have one big memory on him: our father. Paul was only three when our father left us. I remember him as an actual person in our lives. For Paul, he is a name on a birth certificate.

So maybe the explanation for why I had those pine trees cut down was that I couldn't bear to leave them behind while they held the potential to be a house. I must have known deep in my heart that I was about to enter another unsettled period of my life when homes would slip out from under me as they did in my boyhood and I would be on the move again. In any event, the trees came down and yielded an impressive amount of lumber—a seriously big pile of wood.

At this point in the dream, the one that cracked, Paul was already ensconced in his suburban life, having himself recently ended a long relationship and begun another. He brought his five children into his new marriage. His new wife brought three. I was his best man. There was a Catholic wedding followed by life in the big house with the lawn and all the kids. It was right about then that he offered me a patch of his backyard to store the lumber. This would have been 1996. You might say we were both in transit: he into a marriage, and I on the way out.

It still amazes me that Paul never had the mess of wood hauled away to make room for a shed or more grass in his subdivision, an Iowa of lawns. His neighbors in their supersized colonials could not have been pleased with the woodpile and its perpetual halo of tall weeds, which caught leaves, papers and the occasional plastic bag. Yet it was always there—under snow or sodden leaves, depending on the season—when I came to visit him for Christmas, Easter or Thanksgiving.

After the trees had been cut and my wife and I sold the house and our fifteen country acres, I soon left Portland, where I had become the newspaper's editor, and traveled to a new job in Philadelphia. We were separated at first, and then divorced. I worked in Philadelphia, at another newspaper, and raised my son, Adam, through high school. Until his graduation, the two of us lived in a small Center City apartment that I did my best to make a home. Adam graduated from high school and went off to college, and I remained in Philadelphia. I was fortunate to be in a new and nourishing relationship by then, but it suffered the strains that accompany a divorce and the conflicts that arise when two people have jobs in different cities. After Adam's departure to college, my job in Philadelphia ended in 2003 with the arrival of a new boss at the paper. I got a severance package and some reassurances about references.

I soon moved to Boston, where I had been hired to be a professor of journalism. I was happy to land on my feet and pleased to be a teacher, something I had wanted to do for a long time. It was good to be back in New England, which was familiar, and almost home. By then, the divorce was fully final, my mother had passed away and my children were adults and on their own: Elizabeth in New York and Adam in Peru, where he had become a Roman Catholic brother. I missed them both terribly, and my mother too. The only things that had seemed to stay in place were the lumber and Paul.

Of course, I shouldn't marvel at Paul's reliability. We had grown up together and moved around together, and he knew something about the meaning of a home, even when it existed only as a pile of sticks destined to be a cabin.

I have been a lifelong fisherman and fortunate to have fished many places in the world. Once, while walking the flats with my fly rod under a bright sun in the Bahamas, I heard a piercing screech and saw a cleft shadow sweep across the water and over a school of cruising bonefish. There was panic in the shallow water, which suddenly boiled with frightened silvery fish. I looked up and saw a hawk between the sun and the water. The fish could not have seen the bird, and I doubt that they had heard its call. They had felt the swift dark wings between them and the sun in the form of a swiftly moving shadow. In their frightened rush to deeper water, I wondered, were they responding to the imminence of death, or to the fear of the emptiness that lurks behind death?

I had been in my new job in Boston for just over two years when, in 2006, I got the news that my uncle Babe was reaching the end of his fight with colon cancer. All of us in the family had called him Babe because he was the youngest of my mother's three siblings. His real name was Thomas, which he definitely preferred to Babe, but to all of us he was Babe. The news of his fast decline had come to me from my aunt Judith in New York City. She was married to another of my uncles, John, my mother's oldest brother. John and Judith had been an emotional shelter for me as I had stumbled through my divorce, offering reassurance and financial help, and their home in the East Village had been a haven for me more than once when my life was in serious emotional tumult. They had a big black sofa that I'd cover with a sheet and blanket and use as a bed. On the phone, Judith told me that she and John were going to New Jersey to visit Babe, who lived in a retirement community with his wife, Ruth. She was direct: this might be the last chance to see him alive. Did I want to come with them? I immediately said yes and took the train from Boston to New York.

I had sensed from Judith that John had been declining—he was in his eighties—but I was shocked when I reached their home, a loft on the fifth floor of a renovated factory building on East Fourth Street whose walls were covered with the art of their friends in the city. John seemed hardly to know me. He was welcoming as usual, and gave me a strong handshake and big hug, but he could not remember my name. He called me by the old Greek honorific *palikari*, or brave young man. (John's parents, my grandparents, were from Greece, and Greek was his first language.) Together we sang the same verse from an old Greek folk song. First once, then twice, then a third time. He seemed unaware that we had just sung it. He was unusually reliant on Judith, asking her frequently what they were planning for the day. As we prepared to leave for New Jersey, he kept asking where we were going. Judith patiently told him we were going to see his brother Babe.

"Babe is very sick," she told him again.

"He is?" John replied.

"Yes. He has cancer."

Tears filled his eyes each time he heard it again.

I returned to Boston, shaken. My mother was gone, Uncle Babe was dying and John was suffering from Alzheimer's disease. I brooded on the passage of time, the loss of family. The description is inadequate but I felt like I was standing in a house in which everything important to me—books, photos, cards given to me by my children—was being carried out by strangers. What soon would be left? How would I recognize my world and find my way without my mother and uncles? Only one of my uncles, Constantine, was both alive and healthy, and he was at the precipice of eighty. I had grown up with no family homestead that I could return to—no familiar porch, or view to the barn or the mountains, no place at the lake that was full of memories. Four years was the longest I had ever lived in one place as a boy, and that was in a home that we eventually lost in a foreclosure. I did not have a single possession from my childhood. These family relationships were all I had brought into my adulthood.

It is hard to account completely for the shadow that then fell over me, but fall it did, and it came down hard. Maybe it was more than the loss of family members—maybe it was the acknowledgment that I had passed my own personal equinox. I was coming to terms with being the generation within the family that stood between the children and death. I was not old, of course, but I had stepped forward in the inevitable succession of generations.

When I was a boy, my grandmother represented the generation that occupied that final position, and it seemed then that it would always be so; for a very long time, my mother and uncles held it; now it was falling to me and Paul. I had survived—barely—the passing of my mother, because I had begun preparing myself for it as a nervous child, rehearsing the pain of her loss. With her gone, how would I survive without the web of family that my uncles represented? Or a worse thought: I knew I could not survive a world without Paul. He figured too importantly into my recollecting and possession of a past, and he was the one person I could rely on for coherence. We had shared a childhood, and the things that were important to me, the things I could not retrieve—my mother, father, stepfather, holidays, disappointments—belonged to Paul too. He was my link to my past, and that past was at the core of who I knew myself to be.

When I returned from New York, I thought of the hawk, contemplated the shadow that had fallen over me and brooded yet more on the past. Suddenly, memories of growing up took on a powerful and unhealthy importance to me. I felt like I needed to hold on to them to hold on to myself. I leaned against them the way a drunken man might lean against a wall. I recognized all of this as morbid thinking, and I knew myself well enough to realize that I was falling into a familiar abyss. It was as if the ground were giving out from under me. I smiled for my students and diligently put marks on their papers, but the shadow pursued me along the streets of Kenmore Square and in the corridors of the university building where I taught on Boston's short winter days. Neither had the trouble in my new relationship gone away—no one's fault, and not for lack of love, just the reality of two adults juggling far-flung jobs and responsibilities. I didn't have my feet firmly under me.

I had waited out the darkness before. It took longer than a cloud—or a hawk—passing in front of the sun, but it was not dissimilar, and I knew it could be done. One of the benefits of getting older is that you recognize your antagonists and know how to defeat them, or at least give them the feint until they pass of their own accord. I got prescriptive with myself. There were things I could do that had worked before—get some exercise, engage with a pleasant and absorbing task, put myself in a setting that would give me a lift. Maybe I just needed a vacation. I thought of the Florida Keys. I loved the blue water, green cays and sparkling light.

With manufactured optimism, I also decided that part of what I was feeling was simply my inability to be satisfied without some work to do with my hands. I'm happiest when I have a project—a boat to build, a desk to refinish, dinner to prepare. I even enjoy untying stubborn knots in a fishing line. My daughter says I have attention surplus disorder. For no particular reason other than the joy of it, I once spent the better part of a year learning ancient Greek so I could read Plato. I convinced myself that my attention needed a happy and absorbing target and real work, and the depression would lift.

I went down into the basement of my apartment building and rummaged through my storage bin. I took stock of what I had there—again, the obsession with memories—but also inventoried the outdoor gear I had managed to keep through the disorder of the last few years: skis, snowshoes and fishing equipment. I had derived an awful lot of pleasure from these pursuits in the past.

The outdoors had always been good for my soul, and more of the outdoors, combined with some physical activity, might just be what I needed. Trees filtering sunlight or water rushing over mossy rocks—they had worked their healing power on me before. There I was in the city, moving between my second-floor apartment and the university's urban campus, and the closest thing to nature in my life was the nearby arboretum with mothers pushing monstrous baby strollers along asphalt paths and dog walkers stuffing their hands into plastic bags to pick up dog shit. A city park is not the outdoors. I figured some of what I needed to do was get back to that part of me that thrived in nature. I collected my fishing gear and began to prepare for the spring opening of the trout season. It brought back some of the boyhood pleasures of anticipation and absorption. The first day of trout season had always been a kind of second Christmas for me. It was a long way off, but I could still tie flies, assemble equipment and plot trips.

One thought led to another, and soon several strands of what had been occupying my thoughts—fishing, the satisfaction I got from making something, a chance to gather together what remained of my family—began to fuse into a project. Wouldn't it be nice to have a cabin in the woods? Surely, I thought, a cabin would be plenty of project for me. It would put nature—wild nature, real nature, not citified cut-grass and dog-shit nature—back in my life. In a way, it would be a cameo of the bigger effort I was making to put my life back together after a decade of loss and change.

Yes, a little retreat in the woods: it would be just the thing. It filled me with pleasant thoughts. I liked the idea of fitting together posts and beams to make a snug cabin, and there was always the knowledge of the wood sitting in Paul's backyard. I had enjoyed working with Paul before, when we had built the house. I had found the simple task of making a mortise and tenon joint to be a satisfying and complete experience. There was the heavy forward feel of the mallet in hand, the sharp clean edge of the chisel and the fragrant pine shavings that came up from the timber. I loved the way that two and then three pieces of wood fit together to make a solid corner post. It was honest and healthy work. It roughed the hands and rebuilt muscles. I would be outside, breathing woods-scented air. If the day was hot, I could drink cold water from a jug; if the day was cold, I would pull on a wool sweater. All of this struck me as immensely right and necessary. Once the cabin was complete, or so my reverie went, I could bring family and friends for holidays or weekends, or I could use it as a wilderness retreat to be with myself if that was what I needed.

All of this was hovering within me as not much more than a pleasant daydream until early one evening in September 2007. I had come home from the office and went to pick up a few groceries for dinner at the neighborhood supermarket. As I was approaching the register, I grew light-headed, and then I felt the sensation of a bird beating its wings in my chest. In seconds, the bird was flapping madly. I was dizzy and disoriented. I tried to swallow. My throat was tight. I couldn't push the saliva down my esophagus.

At Massachusetts General Hospital, I was put on a gurney and hooked to an IV tube and heart monitor. A nurse took some blood. The test came back rapidly, and a doctor told me there was no trace of the protein that would indicate that I had suffered a heart attack. It was a case, he said, of atrial fibrillation, a flutter of my heart's left atrium. "Have you had this before?" he asked. I told him it was my third experience in eight years. "Getting to be a habit, I see," he said, which I took to be medical humor.

I was in no danger of dying once the doctors had administered a blood thinner, which prevented a clot from forming in the blood that might pool in my misfiring heart. The hazard presented by a clot is in its possible trip to the brain, where it can lodge and cut off the supply of oxygen. This, of course, is a stroke. The doctors— and there seemed to be a growing number of them, including interns, that gathered around my bed each day—were reassuring, but they warned me against a recurrence. In the two previous incidents, and in this one, too, the A-fib had been preceded by a period of anxiety. Each occurrence had increased the likelihood of another. In times of major stress, my heart was learning to slip down a well-beaten path toward arrhythmia.

For the better part of a week, the doctors and I waited for my heart to stop tapping out its distress signal. I sat in the hospital bed and looked out a big window that framed a blue stretch of the Charles River beyond Beacon Hill. Water has always made my mind wander. As sailboats skimmed the surface of the Charles and salt water dripped through a tube into my right arm, I spooled back to those cool late September days when I was a boy of thirteen in South Jersey. Barnegat Bay would flatten under a thin blue sky, and I would row out with long wooden oars to catch a few of the snapper blues that were left over from the August run. It was a good memory, the sun on my shoulders and the red-and-white bobber racing over the wavelets whipped up by summer's last breath.

In the present, though, the heart monitor continued to beep an irregular rhythm. My heart refused to end its tantrum. It wanted to be heard. It had a message. A hospital gives you a lot of time to listen. The idea of getting back to my first self began to seem more important.

In a world that hadn't seemed entirely reliable or kind these past few years, the memories of the woods and waters of my boyhood were pleasurable, and the notion of the cabin, which I had been entertaining, seemed a natural next-step extension of them. My mind grew calm as I pondered how I might build this cabin. I considered its dimensions, thought about materials and even began, in my daydreaming, to hang fishing rods on its walls. I'd make a big mess of blueberry pancakes for the people I brought there. Many of the feelings I had been sorting through seemed to be converging and shifting for the better.

Then, along with everything else, there was this thought that just appeared from I don't know where: the cabin would be a home of last resort. It would root me in a place. It would be my hedge against that old and irrational fear, homelessness. Maybe that had been the ultimate source of my anxiety, and the message my heart was tapping out through the bars of my ribs: *build yourself a home.*

To the surprise of the doctors, my heart went back to its even beating without the electric shock to my chest that they already had scheduled.

Back at the apartment, after leaving the hospital, I felt stirrings of anticipation and possibility. It helped that it was September, a month I've always associated with beginnings. The crickets whirred in the trees outside my second-floor windows. They seemed to be singing me forward. Isn't it a wonderful thing, that the whir of crickets is the same year in and year out? It is the sound of continuity and coherence. Already I was feeling better. I went to sleep contemplating the woodland scene of a simple gable roof, a screened porch and a chimney pushing up wood smoke. I told Paul what I had in mind. I wasn't far into my explanation when I asked if he could help with me it, and he said he would. The same old Paul.

"Where are you going to get the land?" he asked.

"I have some ideas," I said. "Maine, I hope."

First, I had to contend with a practical matter. I lacked a car. In Boston, I was forced to live frugally. My savings had been wiped out in the divorce, and my professor's salary left me with little extra money to buy a car, but I would need a car if I wanted a cabin, and a car cost money. This is what life in America has come to, I thought: a man who wants a little nature in his life must first find the money to buy a car. My stroke of good fortune came with the sale of a book. The first installment of the advance bought a used car; subsequent installments would get me started on the cabin.

At my computer in my office at the university, I scrolled through the country-property ads. They described lots that were along rivers or beside lakes, parcels that held old apple orchards or were open fields. I focused my search on Maine. I knew it held what I wanted in copious amounts: green hillsides watered by little streams, backwoods ponds, and miles and miles of roads that remained unpaved. An unpaved road had emerged as a necessity in my imagination. Let the dust fly. I wanted to be free of pavement for a few long weekends a year and maybe a month or two in the summer.

As I dodged the Boston traffic, the idea of a small cabin had become a way for me to at least think about nature, to put some tree bark and pine sap into my thoughts if not my life. My step felt a little lighter. I took it as a sign that the cabin was the right prescription for what ailed me. I conjured a cabin small, tight and secure against the wind blowing down from Canada and lit by the yellow flame of a hurricane lamp, squeaking as it swung slightly from a hook on the porch. Logs snapped in the woodstove of my fantasy.

I doodled and made sketches. I spent a lot of time thinking about the porch. It seemed to me a porch elevated a cabin above mere shelter. I was talking cabins and porches with a physician friend at dinner and he said, "Yes, a cabin—and a porch that you can piss off of. I've always wanted one." We agreed that the absence of porches off of which to piss had become a serious deficiency of modern male life. The women at the table groaned.

The prospect of doing the work with Paul—and by extension, his sons—made the labor ahead even more appealing and the feeling right. When I was living in Philadelphia, because of the distance and our responsibilities, I had seen him only a few times a year, usually when I returned to visit my mother, who by then was declining and beset with numerous health problems. Paul— with eight children at home, a new marriage and a demanding job—had taken on the burden of caring for her in those final years. There was also some repairing that I needed to do with him.

So the way I was conjuring it, the cabin was going to be a kind of recapitulation of the first house Paul and I had built, except this time it was going to be done in late middle age and the goal would not be to construct a house for starting out in life, but to put up a place for ourselves, where our sons and daughters, now grown, could come to spend time with us in the out of doors.

As my kids burrowed deeper into their own lives and grew more distant from mine, this seemed to be more my dream than theirs. "You're going to build a what?" my daughter asked me when I told her on the phone about my plan to build a cabin in the Maine woods, maybe deep in the mountains. "How will anybody get there?" she asked.

One day in January 2008, I got an e-mail from a real estate agent that said, "This could be a good property for you. It's rural but not too far out. I believe there is power right at roadside." The price was $32,000. It was a number within my reach. The ad described it as five acres of "mixed woodland." It was near the New Hampshire border, in the lee of the White Mountains and in the town of Stoneham. Stoneham, I would soon learn, had no traffic lights, about a dozen roads and a single small market that sold pizza, live bait and two-dollar draft beers and served as a deer-tagging station. I called Paul and told him I had come across a property that might be right. He agreed to come along.

In the code of northern New England, "mixed woodland" means that the trees that are valuable as lumber or pulp have been removed and the logs turned into boards or paper. In other words, some developer had already extracted the commercial value of the land as a woodlot. I guessed that most of the trees from the parcel I was driving to had by now been turned into paper towels at the sulfurous mill in Berlin, New Hampshire, and were on their way to kitchen spills across America. But it was worth taking a trip to see what was left.

What remained was recreational property—a euphemism for a rocky hillside of mostly second-growth oak, maple and beech scored with the ruts of a logging tractor, but close enough to ski areas and trout streams to attract a buyer who wanted a place in the country. This, of course, was me. I hadn't skied since an accident some years ago in which I departed a chairlift too late and blew out both knees, but I had once been a pretty good fly fisherman and I knew the area was threaded with streams. After a couple of wrong turns that brought us to dead ends and unplowed roads blocked by deep snow, we found it. We recognized the lot by the surveyor's fluorescent ribbons and a path that had been cleared by a logging skidder. With three feet of new snow blanketing the ground, we strapped on snowshoes and paddled up the hillside.

The sun was bright, the sky a powdery blue and the snow glittered like tiny crystals as we climbed the east-facing slope. The woods were silent except for our huffing and puffing. Neither of us was in great shape. Both of us could have stood to lose twenty pounds. The only exercise my work had afforded me was pacing back and forth in front of a classroom. Paul is stockier than I, but neither of us makes a delicate presentation. We both have dark hair and broad faces and mustaches that give us an unintended intimidating look. I remember a friend once remarking, when he saw Paul and me talking privately in the back of a room, "Looks like the Archduke may be in for some trouble."

Our snowshoes bit the snow in small steps and sunk a few inches in the plump fluff as we put our weight down from leg to leg. The snow sighed with each press of the snowshoes. We made a trail of overlapping webbed ovals and followed the flags that marked the property's boundary up the hillside. We crossed a single set of deer tracks, heart shaped and distinct in the snow. Later a bobcat track wended along a trail stitched with the prints of a snowshoe hare. It's no small thing to see the mittened shape of bobcat pad. Both animals had been walking, not running, separated by hours or minutes, and I guessed the hungry cat was stalking the hare. I looked ahead but saw no signs either that the hare's tracks were lengthening into a panicked dash or that the cat had crouched, ears back, to leap. I was taking no sides in the tale in the snow. I simply read it as a poem pressed in the winter page.

I would have been happy to follow those tracks all afternoon. I savored this feeling of being out of doors, of pulling the frigid clean air in and out of my lungs, and of being in a place where nature seemed to prevail over people and pavement. I had forgotten how much I relished just being in the woods. I was sweating from the climb up the hillside. I pulled off my jacket and opened my flannel shirt's top two buttons. Paul, I could see, was looking for a good building site—something flat and accessible to a truck and excavation equipment.

My body cooled quickly. I enjoyed the sensation of hard work and cold air on my chest and back as we continued upward. We walked in single file. I went first. The rabbit tracks disappeared into the stiff parchment leaves of some small beech trees that had been uncovered by the wind. The land and the walk were conforming to the fantasy I had been concocting at my desk, and already my mind was made up. I would make an offer.

"Do you think he would take thirty for it?" I asked Paul.

"You can always give it a try," he replied. "The economy's bad, and he might need the money."

Two weeks later, we returned to meet the owner, Rick Rhea of South Freeport, Maine. He had bought the lot and the adjoining 120 acres a year earlier and subdivided it into eight parcels, which he was selling one at a time. He had partnered with a logger in nearby Albany Township, who worked with a crew and skidder. The combination of land developer (or subdivider) and logger is common in the north country. They make their money by identifying parcels of land that can be logged for additional profit and sold in parts, the sum of which exceeds the price paid for the entire piece. Rick was about fifty, wiry with a temporary smile that struck me as either cold or vulnerable. I couldn't tell which right away. His smile seemed as skittish as a small and frightened animal. It would take me some time to get to know him, and I eventually grew to like him. He was direct and without ornament or affectation. I would later learn that he had clashed with the planning board in town—not surprising given my first impression of him—and there was lingering ill will that eventually would affect my plans. Rick had brought his own snowshoes, made of aluminum and plastic, and the three of us walked a wider circle than Paul and I had on our first trip up the hillside. We followed the same trail but then crossed the line of fluorescent flags to a second lot. It was lot No. 7 on the map Rick was carrying, rolled under his arm. The lot was not quite six acres, a little bit bigger than the first, and it held a site for a cabin that was more distant from the road where we'd parked.

The extra distance suited me. I wanted a place to escape to. I wanted to be in the woods. I didn't even want a driveway. I wanted a long walking path from the road to the cabin. Rick suggested a site for the cabin that was mostly a flat patch of ground with a few spindly firs sprouting through the snow—Charlie Brown Christmas trees. The spot was bounded on one side by a granite outcropping that thrust to shoulder height and on the other by a steep downward slope of spindly hardwoods that fell to the road below.

The trees obscured the road, but I caught a glimpse, beyond, of a flat white expanse that looked like an open field. I asked Rick if it was a farm. No, he said, it was a frozen pond. Little Pond, he called it.

Really, I thought. *Little Pond?*

Ah, that old seductress—water.

"I can offer you thirty," I said to Rick, springing the amount on him without a lot of questions. I figured, why not lowball it? He hadn't mentioned any other offers. Maybe I could save myself two thousand dollars.

I saw he didn't expect the offer, that he had figured I was a real estate shopper and not a real estate buyer. This was evident in the way he had tossed his snowshoes to the ground at the beginning of our walk—as if to say, *More time wasted with some asshole from Massachusetts.* The mention of real money changing hands, though, warmed him up. His smile now seemed less distant, more fixed on his face. We made eye contact and he was searching me for bullshit. He said he would have to talk to his partner. This struck me as a variation on the car salesman routine, and I searched him for bullshit. Already we were quietly negotiating.

A week later, in an e-mail exchange, Rick held firm at $32,000. I knew it was a good price despite my lower offer, so I agreed to it. We set a date for the closing. On February 8, 2008, after the stamping of papers and affixing of signatures, I owned 5.49 acres on a hillside in Stoneham in Oxford County, Maine.

It was the beginning of an arc that would carry Paul and me through two cycles of the seasons, and a sequence of surprises, discoveries and unanticipated transformations in our lives.

CHAPTER 2

PRELIMINARIES

There wasn't much I could do before spring. The land was locked with snow and ice, and the first step in actual construction would be to cut a path up the hillside so we could bring building materials close to where the cabin would sit. The lumber was still sitting in Paul's backyard, unsorted. I envisioned a path that would climb from the road, wend through the trees and reach the cabin in a broad curve up and around the hillside. I wanted something not much wider than a game trail. I imagined it as being hardly big enough to let two or three men walk abreast, a trail padded with dry pine needles and showing the coiled roots of some trees that had muscled through the ground. My hope was that the path would be complete in the spring and the cabin would be closed in by winter. It was an ambitious plan. Everything would have to go just right for it to happen.

The land I had bought was on a hillside formed by the sloping face of a knob that rises on the northwesterly shore of Little Pond. The knob rises gently at first, then steeply—so steeply that it would seem impossible to climb to the top except by grasping branches and bushes and pulling oneself up a single step at a time. I doubt that anyone has reached its crown, though I'm tempted to give it a try one day. I will bring some ropes if I do, and binoculars and a nice lunch. A pocked and buckled road threads narrowly between the pond and the knob. The road is the only year-round passage into a mountain intervale about a quarter mile farther up the road.

My hillside and another heaving of the land—this one uninhabited—directly across the pond form the two sides of an entrance into the intervale. The breadth between these two hills is about the length of a very long home run—the sort that sails over the bleachers and bounces on the street outside the stadium. My knob is unnamed; the heaving across the pond is called Gammon Hill. I have a neighbor who is a Gammon, but I have not yet met him. I have heard the pond called Little Pond, Small Pond, Beaver Pond, No Name Pond, Mud Pond and That There Pond. Some people call it Moose Bog. The moose like it in April, when they come down, after a long winter of dry woody tips, for a spring salad of green pondweed. I guess its size at about six acres. It has marshy edges, and a big beaver lodge on its far side, and two wood-duck boxes that some Samaritan has nailed to flooded dead trees. The pond drains into a brook that finds its way to the grassy meadow of the nearby intervale and eventually to Kezar Lake, about a mile distant.

George Ebenezer Kezar was a trapper who explored this country in the early 1700s. He came up from Hiram, in what was then a southerly town in the Province of Maine, and ran a line of traps to the border with Canada, beginning at Great Brook, which is a ten-minute walk from my hillside. Kezar was famous for his encounters with bears, and one legend has him being buried with one arm—the other lost to a bear that had got the better of him before Kezar dispatched it with a knife. Today the lake, several ponds and a river bear his name. So does a pub that serves expensive Belgian beers in nearby Lovell. It's called Ebenezer's. I spent some evenings there as the cabin was going up.

These intervals are common in the hill and mountain country of northern New England: pleasant interludes of paisley-patterned flatland made fertile either by the overflow of brooks or by the downwash from the surrounding hills that ever so slowly manufacture topsoil from eroding rock and composting vegetation. Topsoil is a scarce and valuable commodity in these parts: as thin as cloth on a rough table, not fathoms deep like the prairie soil of the Midwest. My down-the-road intervale is split by a rushing stream called Cold Brook, which has its beginning in the high country between Speckled and Palmer mountains. I have tested it, and even in summer it runs as cold as a glass of iced lemonade. The brook holds small blue and red flashes of sunlight that are actually wild trout not much bigger than a pinky finger. In that first winter of purchase and discovery, when the brook bubbled around translucent and rectilinear panes of sharp ice, I resolved to one day take the time to find its alpine source. So there was another trip set aside for another day.

Today the intervale bristles with poplar and white birch at its tightening margins, but once it was a settlement of subsistence farms owned by kin families with the names Adams, McAllister and McKeen. They grew beans and corn, kept oxen for the plow and milk cows, and raised pigs and sheep. Walking through that settlement in 1860 must have been a cacophonous affair, with chickens clucking, cows mooing, sheep bleating and pigs grunting. The road to the intervale is called Adams Road. As best I can tell, the Adamses have vanished from town, and there's not much now to mark their former presence except the occasional rusted bucket or farm tool half buried in the woods.

It took me some time to find the Adams cemetery. I knew from the moment that I learned of their past in the intervale that there would be a plot of mossy headstones nearby. Eighteenth- and nineteenth-century life in backwoods New England was a numbing succession of deaths: of children from diphtheria, measles, smallpox, fever, influenza and tuberculosis, and of women from childbirth, loneliness and suicide. A resident in town showed me an old photograph of a husband and wife who lived in the intervale in the late 1800s, and they looked like two strips of dried New England cowhide with expressions that would curdle milk. His worn-out shoes, overalls and sunken cheeks and her determined posture and pulled-back hair suggested a life of continuous labor and loss without complaint or capitulation. The longer I looked at the photo, though, I saw in their gaze an appealing countrified awareness that seemed touched with irony; and as I looked still longer, I saw maybe even a little mischief and carnality. Possibly it was the slightly playful addition of his straw hat, with its round brim and shallow top, and his slouch and suspenders, and there was the frankness that resided in his wife's eyes. Surely something must have just occurred on the cornhusk mattress inside the old house.

The mountain at the terminus of the intervale is called Adams Mountain. In the 1960s, an attempt was made to develop a ski area there. The attempt failed for many reasons—not the least of which is that Adams Mountain faces south into the eye of the winter sun. Its brow caught the warming rays and turned the snow on its slope to ice, which of course ruins the skiing by toppling skiers and breaking bones. In more recent years, it has been a good place to find a deer napping in a bed of beech leaves on a cold November afternoon, catching those same warming rays on its dense gray-brown flanks. If a doily of early snow happens to cover the woods floor, then steam sometimes can be seen rising from the deer's warm and recently vacated mountainside bed.

I had a rough idea of the cabin I hoped to build. I wanted it small and simple and tight to the weather. I wanted it snug. I did not want a shack, and neither did I want a vacation home. The very sound of the words "vacation home" made me grimace. I hate even to see it on the page. I was not looking to pile up possessions or bring expensive diversions into the woods. I did not want televisions, microwaves, toasters, electric can openers, popcorn poppers, food blenders, electric blankets or tchotchkes of any kind. This would be something like a monk's cabin or, better, since I wanted to include books, binoculars, some magazines and a sketch pad, a naturalist's or writer's cabin. The woods would be my diversion, and I would look forward to the dramas of big snowfalls, noisy woodpeckers, new seasons emerging out of old ones, furtive pine marten and summer thunderstorms. I thought of a deck officer's quarters on a sailing ship—a gentleman's space reduced to its spartan essentials: desk, chair, chest, bunk, a wooden box with sextant, glass and compass, a table for reading maps and a few good books. Everything would fit together tightly, and anything loose would be stowed in its proper compartment against rough weather. I was building a cabin because I wanted to pare down and find the me that had been misplaced in life's big and little catastrophes of the last decade. The project would be a move toward integration—not separation, escape or temporary stimulation.

I decided I would not bring power up from the road. I would let Central Maine Power Co.'s lines pass by without planting poles on the hillside or stringing a cable through the trees. Maybe I would admit a portable radio to listen to a ball game on a summer evening. I liked the way a baseball game called on the radio collapsed the universe down to a ball, a bat, nine leather gloves and one person's knowledgeable commentary. I had noticed one day while driving to the hillside that a ball game heard over the radio slowed my breathing, maybe even reduced my heart rate—not a bad thing for a guy with my medical history. A small radio would be a good addition to a cabin. The Internet—well, that was an open question. I liked being able to search for a good curry recipe or refresh my memory on the definition of the categorical imperative, but the Web would be a temptation to distraction and pointless stimulation. I preferred books and the company of humans, occupying their bodies and holding glasses of Scotch in their hands. I was not seeking a virtual experience. In a pinch, I could always drive to the town hall and use my laptop to poach the Internet signal in the parking lot.

Of course all this asceticism and roughing it was environmental ideology, pure and simple, and not all of it intellectually consistent. It surely was not cabin construction. I hadn't yet lifted a hammer or bought a nail. But it was a necessary step, I think, and a pleasant one. A cabin is a courtship and not an elopement.

Through this period, in that first winter, I was filled with the agreeable feeling of anticipating a cabin—the contemplation of assembling and inhabiting it—and not of making any final decisions about the specific details of shape, size and pitch, nor of actual work. Of course, many details passed through my mind, but I was trying them on casually without making decisions. It was the infatuation stage of cabin construction. It was enough for me to sit (or lie) down with the idea of a cabin, to own it and enjoy it, anticipation being the purest pleasure.

But as winter ran down and infatuation matured into intention, I began to feel the need to order my ideas about the cabin's design and get serious about the practical aspects of this big project. I already had sunk $32,000 into it—serious money for me. Despite the deep snow, I was impatient to do something, anything to get started. I took out a yellow legal pad and began a list of tools I would need: framing hammer, finishing hammer, circular saw, wood chisels, mallet, combination and roofing squares, chalk line, nail apron, tape measure, carpenter's pencils, cat's paw, drill, wood bits, four-foot level. I browsed antique tool catalogs and wandered the aisles of Home Depot. With scissors and Scotch tape, I built a cardboard model of a cabin, drew in the windows and wondered if winter would ever end.

I was not unfamiliar with cabins, having had a lifelong love affair with the outdoors, and no doubt each of the cabins from my past would inform the one I was about to build. These earlier cabins had contributed to my sense of what made a cabin a *cabin*, in an ideal Platonic sense, and at some below-conscious level I was probably running through the ontogeny of my cabin experiences, in literature and life, as I planned this one. This project was, after all, partly personal archaeology—the search for an earlier and happier self.

I had stayed in many cabins through the years. There was the cabin at Nesowadnehunk Lake, near Katahdin, made from whole logs that had been peeled and painted brown and topped with a shallow roof. It had four small beds, a cookstove and a flimsy card table for meals. Paul and I stayed there on a fishing trip after building that first house. Then there was my old friend Pete Jordan's hunting camp on the upper Kennebec River. It reeked of boots and damp wool and resonated at night with the snores, farts and slurred sleep-talk of men stacked in bunks like paint cans in a hardware store. Pete had been a commercial fisherman in the 1950s, and he was retired by the time he paid me the compliment of an invitation to the camp. It was no small thing to be invited to Pete's camp during the deer season. I tried to reciprocate by inviting him down to Harvard, when I was a fellow there for a year, and he responded in a handwritten letter that Harvard might be an interesting place but he had hay to cut and bale. It was always first things first with Pete. I admired him hugely for his knowledge of the woods and his generous character, which showed in the love he lavished on his bird dogs, none of which paid his commands the least bit of attention. His cabin was positioned below a high ridge, and I liked the way my eyes were naturally pulled upward as I approached it. I stayed there with my son Adam when he was about twelve.

In my list of lifelong cabins, there is the cluster of four or five in northern Maine that Paul and I and our sons traveled to for about eight years over Thanksgivings when the boys were growing up and old enough to go on hunting trips with us. Those cabins were more like bunkhouses with a sink and stove and innumerable nails angled out of the bare two-by-four studs for hanging wet coats and pants. We never shot a deer on those expeditions, but we enjoyed the trips. They regularly commenced a couple of hours after Thanksgiving dinner with a long car ride from Paul's house in Portland to Aroostook County, not far from the Canada border. We would arrive late Thursday night, and a cabin's single outdoor bulb would have been left on for us, marking the particular cabin we were to occupy. They had names like "The Moose" and "The Brook Trout." The proprietor was Carroll Gerow, a man of medium height, slightly stooped, with big rough hands that seemed proportioned to a person a foot or more taller. In addition to being the owner of the sporting camps, Carroll was a woodcutter, local burgher and businessman and hunting guide, and in the years we knew him he never removed his blue porkpie hat, not even at the long dinner table in the lodge that was also his home. Part of the fun of the trips was mimicking his five a.m. roustings: "Okay, boys, time to get up. Boys! Boys!" Just a few years ago, Carroll was killed by his own woods tractor, run over as he made repairs. I'm sure he died with his hat on. He lives in our boys' memories, and mine, too, and we still get cards from his kind and gentle wife, Deanna. Those cabins stand as proof that inspiration derives from many sources. Nails as clothes hangers had already been incorporated into my vision of a proper cabin.

My first cabin experience had come much earlier, and it was also in Maine. I was fifteen years old, living my outdoor life in South Jersey, fishing and hunting and gaining a reputation as the boy you went to if you wanted to know how to catch blackfish or where to set a duck blind. One day I got an invitation from the stepfather of a friend. Would I like to join him on a hunting trip to Maine? This was beyond my most extravagant imaginings. Maine! The family had just moved from New Hampshire to our part of town, a slowly developing wedge of swamp and piney woods on Barnegat Bay advertised as "Waterfront Living—No Money Down." The stepfather was an odd and silent man—my friend had warned me that he was peculiar but encouraged me to come on the trip anyway.

So in late November we drove fourteen hours north, with an overnight stop in New Hampshire for provisioning—mostly, as I recall, beer and whiskey at the state liquor store—and to pick up my friend's grandfather, Cula, who everyone called Bump. So there was the stepfather, whose name was Maurice, my friend Jay and Jay's grandfather, Cula, and me. (It was Bump, deep into his seventies, who consumed most of the beer on the trip, while Maurice drank the whiskey.) Our destination was Hainesville, a crossroads where Maine potato country meets the big North Woods. We arrived at our cabin late one frigid night; it was one big room with a massive old-fashioned cookstove along one side, and, on the other, a collection of beds with broken springs and cloth mattresses about as thick as your average dictionary. The sag of the mattresses was such that a forceful roll in the night would give you contact with the floor.

The temperature was in the single digits when we pulled in, and the snow was deep and frozen. Bump stuffed some newspaper and kindling in the stove. With a fire roaring and the stove sucking air through its many cracks, one side of the cabin reached about ninety degrees while the side with the beds hovered just below freezing. Bump's genius was to find the precise location between the stove and the beds that kept his beer, stacked in cases nearly to the ceiling, at the right temperature for consumption, maybe ten degrees above lake ice. I also remember a wooden door, some tar paper fixes on the outside walls, a sloped floor and tiny windows.

It was late, but not so late that Bump was inclined to cancel the round of visits that were a ritual on arrival. Bump had brought with him gifts he intended to distribute to his local friends. One was Joe MacDonald. Joe was a woodcutter who hauled his logs out of the woods with draft horses, two big Belgians that, I was told, we would use to pull our deer out of the woods if we were to shoot one. This was more than I could take in. We would drag our deer behind a logging horse! We arrived in Joe's driveway, and in the headlights I saw what looked like a fox hanging from his clothesline. And indeed it was: a dead fox awaiting skinning. Two clothespins held the rear paws to the line and the animal looked like it had just left the high dive.

We piled out of Maurice's car, a big Buick, and knocked at the door. It eventually was opened a crack by Mrs. MacDonald. Joe was not home, she said. Where was he? Bump asked. Mrs. Mac-Donald was saying something quietly to Bump when we all heard a terrible yelling and banging coming from inside. It sounded like a wild animal was loose. Mrs. MacDonald stepped from the door toward the crashing, which allowed us to see inside to another door that was bulging as if a bear were pressing against it. The commotion was coming from behind the door, which apparently led to a basement. This was enough information to allow Bump to discern the situation. Joe, it seems, was a heavy drinker, and had even been known to put down a bottle of the liniment he used on his Belgians. When he got drunk he was impossible to control, and Mrs. MacDonald would lock him in the basement. Bump suggested we depart, but first, to my astonishment, he left a bottle of Canadian Club in a bag with Mrs. MacDonald. "This is for Joe," he said.

Our next stop was a broken-down shed house at the end of a woods road occupied by a wisp of a man named Earl Lovejoy. Earl received us with a smile, and we entered into a room that was more hovel than human habitation. There were pieces of chain saw, car parts, gas cans, shovels and wood tools scattered about, and among all of this a swarm of scraggly kittens was tumbling and playing with a rag. Earl was about five and a half feet tall, twisted and bent from the waist, which made him look like he was constantly leaning over to pick something up, when in fact he was unable to straighten himself out. He had wild oily hair, and on both hands he had a total of six fingers, not evenly distributed. Beer cans were immediately popped, and after Bump gave Earl mittens, cigarettes, a flashlight and some wool socks, a conversation about the condition of the deer herd began. It seemed that there were a few deer around, but the numbers were down because of the previous year's heavy snow. The room was poorly lit, by one bulb at the end of a cord that hung from the ceiling, though Earl proudly made note of the fact that he now had "hydro." In the car, on the way back to our cabin, Bump filled Jay and me in on Earl's tragic history: he had lost his entire family, a wife and four children, in a canoeing accident on a nearby lake and had never emerged from his grief—a grief so powerful it had turned him into a child.

On the afternoon of the last day of our hunt, Maurice put me in a place where a deer might cross since it was his plan to make a loop around a nearby swamp. He assured me he would come back to this spot and we would walk out of the woods together on the logging road we had come in on. I was without the slightest sense of where I was. It was bitter cold, and we had three hours of light left in the day. The woods would go black when the sun dropped below the hills, around four p.m. So there I waited, and shivered, and waited, either for a deer or for Maurice.

Soon the sun dropped behind the trees, and Maurice had not come back. At sunset, the temperature fell further, and fast. I put my gloved hands in my armpits. In time, it was completely dark, and Maurice had not returned. I was worried, close to a panic. Had I misunderstood his directions? Was he having trouble finding me? Should I try to make my way out of the woods on my own? I considered firing the gun to signal for help. I got colder and more frightened. My hands and feet felt frozen. Maybe the best thing to do was to let out a yell. If Maurice was nearby and searching for me, he would hear me and holler back. We would find each other. But it seemed a kind of personal failure to yell—after all, I had a reputation back home as a boy of the woods. What sort of woodsman yells for help because it's dark? What would I yell? I decided that I would holler out his name, which was better than calling for help. So I did, and as I did, I saw him leaning against a tree, smiling. He had been there for who knows how long, just watching me be afraid.

Maybe it was this first cabin experience that planted Maine in my imagination as a source of wilderness and personal testing, a place to which, for many reasons, I eventually would return again and again. I am still sorting out the reasons. Each time I returned I was a slightly different person, but surely the reasons included an intuition that nature was a path toward discovery. And maybe, too, I nursed a stubborn need to face down an old fear, one that had developed long before I met Maurice, and that was the fear of being abandoned and lost.

From the beginning, I had thought of the cabin as four walls and a simple roof to shield the rain—that wooden box. Of course, boxes are fine things. I have always been drawn to them—music boxes, pencil boxes, jewelry boxes, shaker boxes that fit one inside another. They have hinges, drawers, nesting lids and doors. A box creates order by enclosing and taming space. A sonnet is a kind of box. So is a symphony.

The nature of the box that would become my cabin depended on the answer to a series of questions:

How would its walls, floor and roof convert the open air through which birds flew into the captured space that was appealing shelter?

How would its pieces be stacked, joined and fastened to withstand wind, weather and gravity?

What materials would be employed?

Would the box have six surfaces—a cube with flat top, bottom and four sides—or would it have ten, twelve, fourteen or more surfaces? A roof alone presents numerous possibilities. A simple gable roof would make a cabin of seven surfaces—folded roof of two sides, bottom and four walls.

Considering these possibilities took me through the end of winter. I looked at a lot of books with photographs of cabins in

Montana, Minnesota, Norway, Nova Scotia and California. They were designer cabins with polished logs, wraparound porches set with Adirondack chairs painted in primary colors and spacious living rooms hung with elk antlers and Navajo rugs. Some of the cabins had kitchens with granite countertops, stainless steel refrigerators and track lighting. The only thing lacking was Sacagawea in six-inch heels. I thought of these books as cabin porn, a mix of money, fantasy and access to nature as a marker of status. This was not the direction in which I was headed.

To put me back in the right frame of mind, I reread books by that old cabin dweller, eccentric ornithologist and Adirondack trout fisherman, John Burroughs. It helped me get right again. His relationship to the woods was direct, his prose and life unadorned and his observations precise and utilitarian. He measured rainfall, noted the dates of the appearances of frogs and named the birds he observed in the trees.

I saw the construction as a series of steps to be taken in sequence. I would go from the ground up, and the outside in. They were:

1. Foundation
2. Frame
3. Exterior siding
4. Roof
5. Interior siding and finish
6. Plumbing, heating, lighting and cooking

Early on, I had decided against a cabin made of logs. A well-built log cabin is a marvelous thing to behold, and it makes sense if you are good with an ax and have access to stands of big straight trees. They are emblems of frontier America. But they have their drawbacks—they are drafty and cold and best when kept small, and they require equipment or many men to lift the heavy green logs. These logs can be laid up round with notches or made square with an adze; in either case, they require caulking to keep out the wind. For me, a log cabin would also mean excluding the big timbers I had saved for so many years. They would become unnecessary given that the log walls would support the roof. I like log cabins; I just didn't want to build one. Maybe someday I will take one on. It would be an absorbing challenge with old tools. I could use it as a backcountry camp for a day or two at a time in deep winter.

My idea for the cabin's foundation was a set of concrete piers set in the ground. They would be cheap, easy and effective. Resting on the piers, the cabin would hover over the earth by about two feet. The floors would stay dry, and I would have room enough to store a canoe underneath in winter. I didn't yet own a canoe but surely would in time: a cabin demands a canoe. The only thing simpler than piers would be to rest the cabin on flat rocks set and leveled on the ground. Some of the old outbuildings in town were built just that way. I would have taken that approach if I didn't fear the heaving of the ground from frost in the spring. Looking back, I wish I had done exactly that.

The frame was a more complicated set of decisions. The pile of lumber in Paul's backyard was still covered with snow, and we had yet to sort it. At this stage, in March 2008, I still didn't know fully what materials I would have to work with, though I had taken a few quick measurements to get a sense generally of the lengths of the beams. Of course, Paul and I eventually got to the pile in the fall, on the sunny day in September, and when we did, we made a list of the timbers we could salvage based on their dimensions and joinery, the ways in which they had been cut to fit together. It was essentially an inventory of our building materials. I wanted to work with what I had, and I hoped not to have to cut them, nor supplement them with additional big-dimension lumber from the lumberyard. We would fit them together and raise them up as if we were raising a barn. Or so I hoped.

The benefit of this sort of timber-frame construction is twofold: the beauty of the frame is exposed to the interior, and the frame carries the weight of the roof on the outside walls, which creates open interiors by eliminating the need for inside bearing walls. It is the method of construction that makes possible the vast interior spaces in old barns and New England's colonial churches. Of course, I did not have in mind anything remotely close to a barn or church, but I would employ the basic materials and concepts of barn construction to create a cabin with an open interior and the warm and abundant feel of wood. With a timber frame and lots of big windows, I reasoned, I could bring the outdoors inside the cabin.

The fundamental unit of timber-frame construction is the "bent." This is an assembly of timbers fashioned into the shape of a raised H—two vertical posts connected near their tops with a horizontal beam. The timbers are joined by mortises and tenons, which are pegged, not nailed. The bents are constructed on the ground (or floor) and raised into place in succession to make the frame of the box. One need only look at the frame of an eighteenth-century church in Boston or Newburyport to see that I'm over-simplifying, but that H is essentially the unit that locks together to make a frame and carry the roof. The old-time housewrights elaborated on this theme in extraordinary ways to create soaring steeples, wide worship halls and multi-tiered barns of enormous capacity.

I had made some sketches of a rectangle—the width of the cabin would be sixteen feet, because that was the length of the timbers that I had to form the horizontal line of the bent, the H. For efficiency and a pleasing appearance, the cabin's length must be in proportion to the width. There's no classic golden mean for cabins, but a design that is too long would turn the cabin into a bowling alley, and a design too short would sacrifice potential living and storage space. The timbers that I had to connect the freestanding bents, one to the next, were eight and ten feet long. Their lengths would establish the distance between the bents and ultimately—adding them together—the length of the cabin. So the length would be some combination of eight and ten. I struck on twenty-six feet—four bents spaced, after the first, at ten feet, eighteen feet and twenty-six feet.

For the walls I decided to use two-by-four studs between the posts to provide a nailing surface for the interior and exterior materials and as a way to hang batts of fiberglass insulation. I had done it this way before, when I had built the house for my family, and knew the process and materials. I went with the familiar.

Then there was the problem of the rafters, the sloped timbers, front and back, that meet to form the peak of the roof and, at the other ends, the eaves. They transfer the weight of the roof to the outside walls. My early and quick inspection of the wood pile told me that the posts and beams were mostly sound, but some of the wood rafters I had hoped to use were questionable. It was essential that the roof framing be strong, safe and reliable. To have a rafter snap would be a catastrophe. I knew I would have to be ruthless in culling any bad rafter material. I decided it would be a good idea to fortify the roof framing by placing standard lumberyard trusses between the big timber rafters. These additional trusses would carry a lot of the roof weight and provide a surface for nailing the boards that would eventually become the ceiling of the cabin.

So, with both the wall assembly and the rafters, I would make use of the big timbers but supplement them with lumberyard materials. I would fit the old lumber into the frame of a new structure. It was not pure timber-frame carpentry, and the serious wood butchers—the guys with Amish-style beards, canvas aprons, and German-forged chisels—surely would mutter, or worse, at my approach; on the other hand, there was reassuring continuity in this method that allowed me to use the old rafters, even if I had to bastardize the frame to force the metaphor. Anyway, it would make a safer building.

For the siding of my timber-frame cabin, I had several choices. I could use clapboards, which are beveled pine boards somewhat less than an inch thick, the one above lapping the one below and showing four inches to the weather. This siding makes the classic look of the New England cape or saltbox, and it was a little too finished for my taste in a cabin. I could use half-log siding, which is nailed with the flat surface of the log to the wall. This would create the impression of a log-built cabin, but it would be a false impression, and that held no appeal to me. Paul had suggested rough-sawn boards cut from unsquared logs, which would result in a wavy edge. They would give the cabin a frontier look—or maybe the facade of some ski-area brewpub.

I poked around town, looking at camps and boathouses. I noticed that most of them used a simple pine-board siding that was milled with a cove along one edge. It is a common siding for Maine lakeside camps, practical and Doric with only a slight flourish. I liked it and found that a nearby lumberyard had it in ample supply. It was my choice.

The roof surface was a settled matter. From the beginning, I wanted a green metal roof. It would last forever and I would get my overhead timpani.

On a piece of graph paper, I fiddled with the design, and hoping that I would have an abundance of eight-foot timbers, I added an ell for additional space. It would come off the front and, if you were facing the cabin, would be on the right side. An ell added a bedroom and spatial texture, though, as Paul reminded me, it seriously complicated the roof. The cabin now would have two roofs, connected at a right angle, forming a valley at the line of intersection. I would need his help figuring out the framing of the valley. I worked out a floor plan with spaces marked for a kitchen and bathroom (left, facing the cabin) and writing room (with bunks) and storage room (right, still facing the cabin). In the middle was living space with a woodstove. The entire ell, ten feet long and sixteen feet wide—those salvaged sixteen-foot timbers being decisive—was the cabin's biggest private room—bigger than both the bathroom and writing room. I e-mailed the plan to Paul. He e-mailed me back, "Getting there. I think I'd decrease the bathroom and kitchen two feet and increase the writing room and closet by two feet."

These were good suggestions, and I made the adjustments. I left undecided how I would handle my water system. My guiding principle all along was to keep everything cheap and simple, and I was considering ways of employing a raised cistern, which might be filled with rainwater or groundwater pumped from a shallow well. If the cistern was set high enough, the water would flow into the cabin's sink, shower and toilet. The cistern could be built on a platform outside the cabin like one of those old-time railroad water tanks, or it could sit in the cabin, above the bathroom. I let the decision stew for a while.

Once the snow had mostly melted from the hillside in late April, Paul and I went up to take some measurements.

The hillside had come with an important restriction. Nothing could be disturbed within 250 feet of the pond. The state had designated Little Pond and its surrounding marsh as critical wading-bird habitat. It was home part of the year to Canada geese, wood ducks, rails, gallinules, herons and cranes. The conservation restriction was fine with me; I was pleased, in fact, that it was in place. I had no need or desire to disturb the woodland below the cabin. The pond was a piece of the landscape that I looked forward to exploring. I was intrigued by the beaver lodge and the mounds of feeding sticks the beavers had scattered around the pond as food caches against tough times. In the early spring the pond wriggled with pollywogs, and already long-legged water striders were skimming over its surface. I was curious to see if I could catch a fish in the pond someday, maybe a small bass or even a trout that had come up from the brook below. I had no desire to harm what would be for me one of the treasures of cabin life that I knew would take me years to fully understand and appreciate. It was one more project I set for myself—a survey of the pond. I would collect leaves, make sketches, take measurements and conduct an inventory of species.

But once I had measured off the distance from the pond's edge up the hillside, I was presented with a problem. The restriction allowed a path to be constructed up the hillside, within the 250-foot zone, but a turn-in to the eventual building site would have to be above the 250-foot mark. Again, fine, except that, at 240 feet, a long granite ledge thrust up from the ground and ran along the edge of the property. Turning in anywhere near the 250-foot mark would require blasting the ledge, and that would be expensive and difficult, and would blow a big hole in the landscape. I was sick about it. I wanted my presence on the hillside to be light and harmonious, and now I was having a serious discussion with Paul about backhoes, pneumatic hammers and dynamite. Maybe I had not done my due diligence and the purchase had been ill-considered. I could sell the land, I thought, and still get out of it without a loss.

Paul and I walked up and down the right-of-way and took more measurements, but we could not figure out a way around the ledge. There was only one way in, and the ledge was a good forty feet of granite obstacle preventing it. It was blast, back out or seek an exception to the no-disturb rule. I doubted we could get an exception. Paul, who often encounters construction impediments in his work, said it might be possible. We talked it over and decided to play it out. Paul made a telephone call to the Department of Environmental Protection, then followed up tenaciously with e-mails through the spring to environmental officials who had questions. It was a reasoned back-and-forth with references to distances, environmental buffers and intrusions. Finally, he received this note: "You may proceed with your plans to develop that path to the cabin site as proposed. No further permitting will be necessary as the proposed path is not likely to have a significant impact on the adjacent wildlife habitat buffer."

The experience certainly debunked all the loose talk that gets thrown around about the inflexibility of bureaucrats and environmental regulations. Now that I knew I didn't have to blast, I went looking for an excavator who could cut in the cabin path. These men are spread across most of rural America. With backhoes and dump trucks they dig foundations, clear paths, construct driveways, plow town roads in winter and clear culverts in the fall. Sometimes to make a living they combine their digging and hauling with concrete foundation work and carpentry. They usually carry big debt on their equipment, their lives are noisy and hot (or sometimes very cold), and more often than not they have dirt in their shoes, but they are their own bosses with their own businesses. Their wives do the books, and somehow they get their kids through college. The difference between a good month and a bad one might be having a few guys like me showing up in town wanting to build a place in the country.

I called three excavators, and all of their estimates struck me as high. I soon learned why from the excavator who had given me the lowest price. In the aftermath of Rick Rhea's dealings with the town's planning board and the ill will that had developed between them, the town had increased the minimum driveway width for newly subdivided property to twenty-four feet. The town could not do much about Rick since he had prevailed in his division of the property, but it could be tough with the people who bought his land, and the twenty-four feet that the ordinance required might settle the score. It was heavy-handed—wider than many of the roads in town. Not only would the new width add expense to my project before I had even gotten started on the cabin, it would disturb the hillside, perhaps even more than blasting the ledge. I would have to give up my dream of a narrow trail from the road to the cabin. I had wanted the cabin to disappear among the trees, to fade among the grays, browns, blacks and greens of the trees and rocks. A twenty-four-foot driveway would be a big gravel scar up the hillside. And there was more: the town's part-time code enforcement officer thought I should also have a forty-foot turn-around on the hillside at the top of the drive, to accommodate a fire truck. I was looking at the construction of a parking lot.

I put my head in my hands. I had settled on the excavator who offered the lowest price, an earnest young man in town who was also a builder. We were discussing the code problems when he let me know that he was a member of the town's planning board. Why hadn't he told me this before? This was a stroke of major good fortune. He even agreed that the width rule was unreasonable. I asked him if it would be useful for me to appeal directly to the town by making an appearance at a planning board meeting. He blew some air skeptically through his lips, not quite a whistle. He shook his head in indecision. He was not so sure it was a good idea. Probably not, he said. I was from out of town—Boston, no less. There was still a lot of heartburn over Rick Rhea. We talked the problem through further, and I perceived that he had his own dispute going with the board, the exact nature of which I could not grasp. He was telling me, obliquely, that his problem with the board might attach itself to my problem with the driveway. I would be wading into complicated town politics and personalities. I decided I should give it a try anyway.

The planning board met in the back of the town's fire station. I had called ahead and asked to be put on the agenda. On the evening of their meeting, I waited for my turn, the only nonmember in attendance. Seated around the table were a woman and four men. The youngest was in his twenties, my excavator, who was trying to aid my cause by not making eye contact with me; the oldest was in his seventies, a small and wiry man with a T-shirt that read "Kiss a Moose." The board's chairman, a person I knew to be an attorney from a little research I had done ahead of the meeting, noted my presence and told the group that I had asked to speak to the board, which gave its assent.

I introduced myself, thanked them for the opportunity to address them and explained my situation. I had bought a piece of land in town, wanted to put up a cabin and hoped to do so without disturbing the natural setting, but had come up against the wide driveway regulation. I asked, respectfully, if it might be waived to allow a narrower drive, maybe twelve or fourteen feet, which was common in nearby towns. Somewhere in my discourse I acknowledged the board's authority and the importance of its work and complimented the town on its beautiful setting among the hills and lakes. There was silence when I was done. I could feel them sizing me up. Maybe they thought if they looked hard enough they could see into my real self and real intent. The specter of Rick Rhea loomed in the room. I broke the silence and said, with some earnest enthusiasm, that I hoped to be a good neighbor.

This was true. A debate ensued. Some expressed their concern about the entire way the land had been subdivided in the first place; another worried about a precedent for other lots up on the hill; still another pointed out that a wide driveway would be necessary for a fire truck to turn around. I felt the discussion trending against my request, and I was powerless to stop it. It would be impolitic to interrupt their deliberation once it had begun. I had had my chance to speak. I was going to be stuck with twenty-four feet. The oldest member of the board, the one wearing the "Kiss a Moose" T-shirt, finally spoke. He had been silent until then. He unscrewed himself from the posture he had been in, legs crossed in one direction and torso turned pointing in the other. They all shifted to hear him. Even before he had begun, I could see that he had taken the taut coil of his body and was transferring its energy to what he was about to say.

"Damn it," he said. "The man wants to build a camp on property he bought. He paid money for it." It was clear that he was unleashing outrage over the state of the nation as he had come to judge it from his perch as a lifelong and tenth-generation resident of Stoneham; to him, my problem with the regulation was only the latest example of the sorry state of the country. "If it's okay with him that a fire truck can't get up there to turn around, and it burns down, well, that's his problem. I say let him do it."

The man had authority. His reasoning settled on the board like a gentle snow. After a little silence, I could hear it being processed in the light hum of conversation. It was hard to refute: good country sense, they thought. His money, his cabin, his fire, his loss. Besides, he doesn't look like such a bad guy. Okay, they agreed as a group, I could go ahead and build a narrower driveway, but it would be provisional and need approval of the town's residents at the next town meeting in March. Everybody in Stoneham would get to vote on my driveway. I thanked them and happily made my way home to Boston.

In May, with the hillside showing new leaves, Paul and I met my young excavator at the base of the right-of-way on Adams Road. We planned to walk the intended path of the driveway and establish the site of the cabin. Paul brought with him his son Paulie and his three-year-old grandson Maddik, who was the son of Paul's older daughter, Katherine. I was struck by how much he looked like Paul as a boy, impish yet with heavy eyebrows. Paul often babysat for Maddik when Katherine was working, and he took him on many of his errands and excursions. Maddik liked to climb over Paul when he was in his big chair at home, watching television or opening the mail, and Paul would lift and spin him overhead. They traveled as sidekicks in Paul's pickup truck.

Paulie was twenty-one years old, long, skinny and furiously tattooed on his arms, chest and back. In another few months, he would leave for Orlando, Florida, where he would attend the Motorcycle Mechanics Institute. Paulie had been a handful for Paul to raise—impulsive and often in trouble at school and with the police—but lovable and irresistible even to the teachers and school administrators Paul often had to meet with about Paulie's behavior. He simply could not sit still in class. He was a jack-in-the-box with ants in his pants. He would get up and walk around in the middle of a lecture. At one point, as a way of keeping him in school, his teachers had decided they would dismiss him ten minutes early from every class so he could go to the gym and shoot baskets to burn off energy before the start of the next class. Paulie had found trouble the way cockleburs find a pant leg. It came in many forms: driving unregistered snowmobiles, tearing around the neighborhood on dirt bikes without mufflers, getting into shoving matches that turned into fistfights . . .

His most prominent tattoo was for his grandmother—my mother—with whom he had been especially close. He'd often drop by with a pizza, which she preferred to the food served at her senior housing complex, or help her from her easy chair to the bathroom as she grew more infirm in her last years. Paulie's preoccupation at the moment was stock car racing. He drove a 1986 Chevrolet Monte Carlo with a 350-cubic-centimeter engine, which he had assembled himself from five or six other cars. Paul had taught him basic auto mechanics in their two-car garage. I had gone to one of his races at a country track near Portland. His crew included a seasoned mechanic and driver, friends from the Portland neighborhood and two girls who were currently working at a local strip club. As a child, Paulie had been present when I had brought the lumber to Paul's backyard all those years ago, and when I had come to visit he would often ask, "Uncle Louie, are we ever going to build a cabin?" Now that it was about to begin, he wanted to be present for the event.

Back in January, when Paul and I had walked the land with Rick, we had trudged straight up the hill, following the right-of-way that had been knocked down by the logger's tractor. This eventually would be the base of the driveway until just shy of the ledge. Then it would turn right and find its way, switchbacking with the lay of the land to its destination, once we had settled on it.

My unnamed knob is a ripple in the runup to the White Mountains. The big peaks, which hold snow into June and sometimes even later, rise up several miles to the west. Still, the hill country surrounding the knob has more than an easy roll to it, and sometimes you have to turn and tilt your head to see the tops of the foothills as you are driving along the state highway from Norway. The knob is seventy-one miles from the sea—a straight line east would touch the coast at Camden, but the natural direction to the sea follows the contour of the land, south by southeast, which is the path the Saco River takes to the Gulf of Maine. The hillside occupies the north end of the Saco watershed. All the water that falls from the sky or gurgles from the earth in a wedge-shaped basin whose west wall is New Hampshire's Presidential Range flows, in a variety of brooks, streams and rivers, to the Saco, and then to the big sandy beaches at Camp Ellis and Biddeford Pool. A watershed is a marvelous thing. It embraces plants and animals at high and low elevations, in swamps and atop dry escarpments, making a natural community through topography, climate and gravity. It provides a metaphor for harmony, diversity and wonder. The rain that would drip off my metal roof might eventually be sipped by a deer in the eddy of some brook twenty miles away, or by a lady serving tea in Biddeford.

The cabin would be about seven hundred feet above sea level, which meant that the average declination to the beach at Camp Ellis would be about ten feet per mile. If I could pull a string from the top of the knob above the cabin to the seaweed lying on the beach at low tide at Biddeford Pool, the line would seem nearly as flat as a billiard table, maybe with the west end of the table propped up with a few dimes. But of course it's not the average declination that matters. The land between the sea and the knob is mostly unvarying coastal plain until you get within a mile or two of the cabin; then it begins to rise, giving the Saco River its quicker upper currents and my hillside its steep slope.

The five us, with Maddik on Paul's shoulders, meandered up the hillside, getting a better sense of its shape and the possibilities for holding the cabin in one of those flat places that seems like a natural terrace. Ferns had sprung up among the trees in the cool dark places along the logger's path, and near the bases of the pine trees mayflowers tendriled along the ground and put out small bursts of white blossoms. The ground was moist underfoot, even a little spongy, still full of snowmelt and spring rain, pulsing water out of old leaves to form small brooks.

We dispersed on the way up the hill, giving the impression of a search party. This was just what we were. We found two or three good sites for the cabin. The places were high and dry, somewhat flat, and two of them afforded a partial view of the pond across the road. After a thorough surveillance, we regathered on a big flat rock, sat and talked it over. We narrowed the choices to two, and then put one over the other because it was closer to the right-of-way and therefore would require removal of fewer trees and a shorter path, which meant less expense and less disruption to the hillside. While the others stayed at the rock and dozed in the sun, I went back to have a second look. I wanted to stand there quietly and alone and open myself to the sight, sound and feel of the spot. Paul had understood and had made no effort to come with me.

I put myself in the place, roughly, that would represent the center of the cabin. My mind ranged over the hillside, in all of its folds, creases and flat places, like a dog looking for a place to lie down.

The site was on the far side and upper end of the ledge we had successfully avoided blasting. It was a kind of small tabletop set within the descent of the hillside, which made it good for building since it would not require scraping to create a flat space out of the hill's slope, and it was more open than the other locations we had considered. A few beech and hemlock trees grew on it, and some spindly striped maples, which in Maine are often called moosewood. There was a stand of tall red pines uphill of the site and slightly back, a good spot, I couldn't help thinking, that I might one day clear for an apple orchard. In a direct line from what would possibly be the front of the cabin, about one hundred yards distant, the hillside showed a gully, down and then up—and up and up toward the knob. Looking in the direction of the road, I caught a glimpse of the silver sparkle of the pond through the new leaves of the red maples and oaks, which mostly covered the cuff of the hillside.

At this time of day, around ten a.m., the sun was over the farthest end of the pond. The sun's arc, I guessed, would drop below the westerly hill behind the cabin at sunset. I pictured the cabin in a variety of positions on the site, turning it in my mind; taking a few steps, I imagined myself standing on the porch at each position. How would the sun touch the cabin through the day and through the year, and what would I see from my aerie among the trees? I looked right and left, down to the ground and up to the sky. I gave all of this considerable thought and felt good about the possibilities. After a half hour or so of these land-sun-cabin speculations, I arrived at the angle at which I thought the cabin should face the downhill slope, which would put the morning sun in the kitchen window four seasons of the year. I liked a cheerful morning kitchen. The cabin would look obliquely down the hillside, at an angle of about forty-five degrees to its descent, so that its front would face east by northeast. Of course, this would mean a porch full of snow after a December nor'easter, but this was what the land presented. There were lots of variables that were in my control, but the position of the knob and the direction of the wind were not among them. These were limits within which I had to work. I was partial to an eastern exposure anyway, and was already enjoying the warmth of the May sun and the thought of myself busy in the sunlit kitchen.

I kicked a heel mark in the ground that represented the center of the cabin. This was the spot. "Only if we are capable of dwelling," wrote the German philosopher Martin Heidegger, "only then can we build." I felt that I had already begun to dwell on the hillside. I knew I would be back for a reconsideration and to become better acquainted with it, in all its rocks and folds, but for now this would be the cabin's location. Of all the cabin decisions I would make, this would be the most important. I walked back to the big rock where Paul and the group waited for me. They were silent and resting in the sun.

"So what do you think?" Paul said.

"I like it," I said. "Let's put it there."

In June, I began my search for used windows and other salvaged building materials. Windows would be an expensive component of my project if I bought them new. A small double-hung window on the low end runs to two hundred dollars, and I needed at least sixteen of them, some of them big. It would be easy to spend ten thousand dollars on new windows. I didn't have that kind of money. I needed to keep the cost of the project low, and I liked the look of old windows anyway. I went to the Internet and found this item among the old doors, kegs of nails, and odd lots of shingles and lumber that were for sale.

> **Used Windows with Frames and Door—$5**
> **(Westport Point, MA)** Fourteen used wood
> windows and one door, with frames. Mul-
> lions 6x6 separate panes and larger. $5 each.
> Double hung. Lots of window sizes. Ideal for
> sheds and outbuildings. Good condition.

I called the owner, encountered a diffident old voice that said they were still available, and drove down to have a look. They were stored at a house on a country road near the beach. They definitely were used, but I liked the old mullions and six-over-six and eight-over-six lights. They would be hard to match in a new window, and they would be way too expensive if I tried. The old windows also had screens. It was still early to take possession of them because I had nowhere to store them yet, but I was concerned that someone else might snap them up. Paul advised against getting them. "You don't have anywhere to put them," he said. I drove down a week later in a rented truck and took them anyway. I knew they would give the cabin a settled and traditional look. The owner had no other interested buyers. I could have them for nothing, he said.

Back in Boston, I stacked them inside the rear courtyard of my apartment building. It was only a matter of time before everyone in my building got an e-mail from the building manager wanting to know whose windows were blocking the courtyard and warning that they would be put out with the trash if not removed immediately. I hit "reply all" to his message and confessed to everyone in my building that they belonged to me. I begged for a little more time before clearing them out. Over the next two weeks, I hauled them in three trips to Maine, on top of and inside my car. Paul looked them over. "I hope you didn't pay anything for these," he said. Of course, I left them in his backyard.

By July, I had the town's permission, an excavator and even windows. It was way past time to get started. I still had a chance to have the cabin closed in by winter if we pushed the work schedule. I wanted to use the next four months to get a lot of the building work done, but just as my excavator arrived at the hillside, it began to rain, and rain some more. We couldn't begin, my excavator told me, until the rain stopped. The ground was soaked. We needed at least three or four days of no rain, or the hillside would turn into a field of mud. So we waited. The rain would stop for a day, then begin again for three or four days. We would get two dry days in a row; then it would rain for six days straight. I kept checking the reports: more rain ahead. It was destined to become the wettest summer on record. It rained fifteen inches; a normal summer in Maine gets about nine and a half. There were local flood warnings.

Eventually the weather turned more favorable for building, at least briefly, but on the days of no rain my earnest young excavator had equipment problems—either the equipment was on the wrong end of town at another job or something was not functioning. (Why, I wondered, was it at another job?) I had been calling him every Friday through the summer to see if he had been able to snatch some time to get some work done when the sun made brief appearances. I usually reached his wife, who said she would be sure he got the message. At summer's end, I still had no drive- way even though the rains had mostly ceased. I was running out of time, and my young excavator was growing more difficult to reach and more diffuse in his commitment to a start date. I saw where this was going—nowhere—so I called him and said I would need to find someone else to do the work. He seemed relieved, but I had lost my summer. I went back to the excavator who I had initially rejected because he had given me the highest price. This time I was a supplicant. I explained my predicament—limited time, need to get started, wanted to have it closed in by winter. I didn't touch my forehead to the floor, but only because he would not have seen my prostration over the telephone. I would have said ten Hail Marys and offered five readings of the Uniform Building Code if he'd asked for it as a condition for starting work. I'd really appreciate it, I told him, if he could get up there soon. After a long moment, he said he thought maybe he could get to it that month, September. His price came in a little higher. This, I guessed, was the premium I would pay for not having se- lected him the first time. I was willing to pay it. He turned out to be as good as his word. He got there rapidly, and I soon had a path to the cabin site.

Hallelujah.

It was late September by then, and I was back to teaching classes at the university, so I could not run right up to have a look as I wanted.

Paul drove up, approved of the work and sent me some photos. By now the leaves on the hillside were just beginning to turn color, and his photos showed a sweeping path tunneling through the oaks and maples and climbing the hillside. It was just as I had pictured it. Double hallelujah. I broke free of university duties on a weekend in early October and drove to Paul's house. We loaded the timbers we had sorted a few weeks earlier onto a flatbed trailer—the one Paulie used to transport his stock car to the track—hooked it to Paul's pickup truck and hauled them to a landing near the cabin site. We were prepared to begin building, finally.

But still we couldn't get traction. Paul and I could not seem to find a weekend in October or early November when we were both free for cabin work. We would need to go up together to lay out the foundation and begin digging the holes for the piers. I was chair of my department at the university, which required me to be present for weekend events, and Paul had commitments at home and church.

Paul's involvement with the church had begun with my mother. She had moved to Portland to be near Paul and me in the early 1980s, when our children were small, and she had become an active member of the city's Greek church. If a building issue arose at church—peeling paint, lack of air-conditioning, crumbling steps—she volunteered Paul. "My son is in that work," she would say proudly, as if she were making a donation, which of course she was. Paul would get a call the next day from someone on the parish council. "Sure," he would say. "I'll have a look." He solved problems and saved the church money. He knew contractors and inexpensive work-arounds, and he got discounts on materials.

But my mother had operated in complex ways, and she rarely

had a single agenda. She was also eager for Paul to baptize his children in the Greek church. Slowly and inexorably Paul was drawn into the church; in time his children were baptized there, and Paul became a member. My mother got her way, and Paul took to it without complaint. He was social and reliable, and soon he was on the building committee, the festival committee and then the parish council. He was also helping some of the old ladies in the church with their homes. He would drop by to examine a wet basement or to fix rickety stairs. The priest saw in Paul someone who had street sense, as well as someone with whom he could talk privately about the people and politics of the church. The priest was a theologian, more comfortable with ideas than with people, and he often grew frustrated with his flock. He and Paul would talk over a situation, and a solution would emerge to whatever issue or conflict the priest had found intractable. And in this way, over the course of about fifteen years, my brother, who had evinced not a single religious sentiment that I can recall in all the years we were growing up, became a pillar of Holy Trinity Orthodox Church.

Until we could get started, I found ways to slip away from campus for a day at a time. I threw jeans, old shoes and a jacket into the car. Faculty e-mails, lamentations and jeremiads would have to wait. The pull of the hillside was too strong to resist. I did not mind the three-hour drive. The prospect of a walk in the woods or around the pond made the time in the car worthwhile especially then, in autumn, the best of seasons. I listened to music on the radio and witnessed the reds and yellows of the leaves become more brilliant as I drove north. October is a lazy month, a kind of dreamy sleepiness falls over the woods. The sun is warm, the air is dry and the cicadas are buzzing in the tall grass. The spicy tincture of wild apples floats on the breeze. No one understood the time of year better than Keats.

SEASON of mists and mellow fruitfulness,
Close bosom-friend of the maturing sun . . .

There is the sharp scent of wood smoke in the mornings as stoves take the chill off country houses, and the happy sight of leaves racing in crazy funnels in the wind across dry open fields. These were delicious sensations. Each time I arrived, I felt as drunk as a horse that has gorged on wild fruit. I was happy to be at the hillside even if there was no work I could do on my own. There is a lot of idle looking and learning that goes into cabin building, too, and I was absorbed in the surroundings and the season whether I had a tool in my hand or not. In a spiritual sense, the project was well under way.

I was discovering something that I suspect I had known since that first winter walk in snowshoes. I wanted to make this hillside my own in the way that the landscape of my boyhood had been my own. The way toward possession, in the best sense of that word, was to learn it, and the best way to learn it was with lots of long walks. I traversed the hill up and down, and sometimes I followed what would be the natural contour lines of rounded hills. Other times I plotted and walked straight lines, from here to there on the map. I sat on stone walls, leaned against the trees, knelt for a closer look at the brooks. I even took the occasional short nap, by leaning against some soft and slightly rotten stump and stretching out my legs. I ran the soil of the hillside through my fingers—it was simultaneously gritty and smooth, a dark pudding of rotten leaves and glacial rock flour—and tasted its bitter twigs.

I had grown up among marshes, sassafras, holly, and scrub pine. The South Jersey soil of my boyhood was gray beach sand—the bottom of an ancient sea. Rocks were so uncommon in that landscape that when people found them they painted them white and set them out as ornaments. By contrast, the Maine hillside was rugged and ledgy, and it coughed up a prodigious amount of rocks. The glaciated soil grows spruce, fir, white pine, beech, white oak and rock maple, trees almost entirely absent from my boyhood. These were two different landscapes, but they shared one powerful attribute: both were manifestations of the natural world—plants and animals and weather and soil and seasons working together to form a coherence of life, breath and natural beauty, and both spoke to me in a common language of metaphor and first principles. I never would be able to score the Maine hillside with the events of my boyhood—I would never be thirteen again and watch ducks come into a Barnegat marsh as the winter sun threw its first light of the day over the dark brackish water, nor would I be able to wade into the green briars and weed fields with my bird dog, Shadrach, to flush bobwhite quail. Those years and experiences were gone. But maybe I could come to know this little patch of hillside well enough to say I understood it. I wouldn't know it as a boy can come to know the woods, because a boy gives himself to it completely, but I could learn it as an adult, by walking and watching and listening. There is no love like the first, and there is no landscape like the one we grow up in, but love has more than one life and I hoped I could possess this landscape with some

of the feeling I had felt for the first. I could not go back and fix
my family, make my father stay or find the money to stop the
foreclosure of our house. Those things were done, and they would
always be done, and the first landscape would always be gone. I
would have to know this place differently, with more deliberation,
experience and tempered hope. Yet there was a strong sense of
return. I thought of the lines by T. S. Eliot:

> We shall not cease from exploration
> And the end of all our exploring
> Will be to arrive where we started
> And know the place for the first time.

One weekend in the late fall, I drove to the hills to soak in the
pensive November atmosphere and reassure myself about the
cabin site, which was still very much devoid of a cabin. I arrived
in the afternoon and made my usual circuit up the path to the
cabin site, and then higher still to the ridge below the knob, and
then down an old logging road to the pond. As I walked around
the pond toward the end of the day, I spotted what looked like a
small bear swimming in the water, except that this bear seemed
to have a canoe paddle lashed to his behind. I went in for a closer
look. It was a beaver, a very big beaver, and when I approached,
it swam three tight circles of exasperation, slapped the water's
surface with its long flat tail and disappeared. I scanned the water
for its reappearance. It showed up a hundred yards farther off,
near the mound of mud and sticks that was its lodge, and then it
dipped below the surface again. I assumed it had entered its tun-

nel and was at the moment inside with its family, all of them wet and smelling very much like beavers and pushing and squeaking and finding a way to be warm and comfortable in their home. Here was a happy family with no thoughts other than a little food and a good long sleep. This was better even than following old bobcat tracks.

I went down on my haunches, Gandhi-style, and took in the tableau of pond, beaver lodge, setting sun and serrated dark line of the treetops. November is a pleasantly melancholy month. The branches of the hardwood trees are bare, and only the beech leaves and clusters of a few stubborn papery oak leaves hang on. Underfoot, the red leaves of the maples are already purple and black and beginning to rot. The smell is pungent, fecund, nostalgic. There is always rain in November, lots of rain, though at that moment the sky was clear with a few high purple clouds. The alders rise from the muddy places as dark gnarled skeletons, their catkins dried up, and the woodcock have departed to the swamps of Louisiana. There is also a quickening in the woods as the animals prepare for winter. The bears range widely and forage for last meals before their long sleep, and the bucks are in their mating rut, lunatic in their pursuit of does. The broods of grouse have dispersed into singles and doubles, and the final flocks of blackbirds pepper the sky. The onset of winter is felt in the cold hardening ground and diminishing light of the afternoon.

All of this was on my mind, as a kind of fugue of sensations, and it made me reluctant to leave the pond. At that moment, my hesitation was rewarded with an astonishing sight. The setting sun flooded the pond with golden light, making it steadily brighter as the surrounding woods seemed to grow darker. It was as if all the light that had been gathering through the day in the nearby mountains was now answering the call of gravity as it drained down to the pond—rills of light flowing into brooks of light that were pouring over glowing rocks, making waterfalls of light, all of which was pouring into the pond, which was now a glowing bowl of light. It seemed on the point of ignition. And suddenly the moment passed. The sun slid below the mountain behind me and the pond went as dark as the hills.

Even though we hadn't yet been able to schedule our first weekend of work at the cabin site, Paul and I were in close communication about the preliminaries, one of which was an important design question, involving the layout of the foundation piers. The piers needed to line up under the girders, which are the principal horizontal supports that run under the length of the floor. The spacing between the piers had to be right: too far apart and the girders would sag or break; too close together and we'd be wasting material and creating extra work. I had three choices for pillars: prefabricated columns, stacks of cement block or Sonotubes, which are cardboard tubes into which cement is poured. Sonotubes were the cheapest and in this instance probably the best choice because we could set them deep, below the frost line. Paul sent me this e-mail as we considered the options:

> There are a couple of different ways to frame out the floor or how the framing relates to the Sonotubes. I will draw you a sketch and e-mail it to you tomorrow. We should decide on which method as it will determine the layout of the Sonotubes. I hope you don't mind my thoughts on all of this.

It's the project manager in me. I'm used to breaking
everything down into pieces. I think this camp and location
is going to be a home run when it's all said and done. I'm
liking that area more and more.

I skimmed the note and lingered on the final sentence and especially the phrase "home run." This was good. I was worried that
I had put him in a position where he might feel trapped by the work
and the extent to which I was leaning on him. The last few times I
had talked to him he had seemed to be in a funk—more than the
usual cantankerousness that came over him from time to time.

As a next step, Paul developed two sets of drawings for the
positioning of the piers. He sent an e-mail to an engineer with
whom he worked on some big commercial projects and asked him
to review the pier, girder and joist options for the cabin. He copied
me on all of these e-mail exchanges, and I enjoyed reading the
back-and-forth with its professional jargon and banter. It gave me
an insight into his manner at work and his competence. "This is
a camp so it doesn't need to be a perfect analysis," he wrote to the
engineer. "No special inspections here."

Near the end of November, we finally found a weekend when
we could get to the hillside together. With the engineer's input,
we had settled on a pier design and marked it on the bare ground.
My excavator had scraped the ground clear of bushes and trees.
We snapped chalk lines and drove stakes. There it was: the size
and shape of the cabin, as a living blueprint stamped on the dirt
and fallen leaves in blue carpenter's chalk. I stepped inside, walked
around a bit, testing out the rooms. I pronounced myself satisfied.
We were ready to set the foundation.

Somewhere along the way, Paul had developed an aversion to using a power auger to dig the holes for the foundation piers, which had been my preference and plan. He predicted it would hit rocks in the ground and be unable to achieve the four feet of depth we would need to sink the piers below the frost line. He suggested I rent a small backhoe. "If you hit rocks," he said, "you will end up having to get one anyway to dig them out." I favored the auger, reasoning that the job would go faster. If we hit a rock, I would simply move the position of the pier and dig a different hole. He was adamant in his opposition to the auger. "You can't do that," he said. The piers needed to be in the right places to bear the weight of the cabin, he explained. I was prepared to risk the small possibility that an offset pier might stretch the span specifications of the cabin's girders. When I said this, he looked at me as if I had suggested we hire monkeys to pack our parachutes.

One of the stories that had been told and retold about Paul sums up his attitude toward shortcuts. He was on his first big construction management job, as the owner's representative at a major office building project in Portland. He was about twenty-eight years old. The day had arrived for a major concrete pour—for the building's footings and foundation to be constructed. A long line of concrete trucks arrived to make their deliveries. Paul decided to check the wet concrete in the trucks for its soundness before accepting it. It was his discretion, and he was going by the book. The quality of the wet concrete is checked with a slump test—a concrete sample is poured into a cone, the cone is inverted and removed, a steel rod is inserted and then the degree to which the concrete slumps is measured against specifications. The sample that Paul had taken from a truck failed the test. It contained too much water, and since all the trucks were carrying concrete from the same mixing plant, he told them he was rejecting all of their concrete. There was nothing for them to do but take it back and dump it, he said. Hell broke loose among the drivers, and the concrete company called the project's owners, furious. Who was the new kid pulling this shit? Paul's decision stood, and the trucks departed and returned with fresh concrete that could pass the slump test.

So I should have known when I suggested a shortcut that his answer would be firm. I rented the backhoe.

We turned up the first ground in November. Late fall is not the usual time to start a building project in the north country, but I was craving this cabin and unwilling to delay it any longer. I hoped we could get a lot done before the first snow. In the meantime, I continued to wonder what was distracting Paul. He seemed a little distant.

CHAPTER 3

LOST LANDSCAPE

By the time you hit your sixth decade, life's losses begin to pile up. If you have been lucky or resourceful—luck being by far the more determinant of the two—the pain of the losses has been reduced somewhat by the satisfaction of the things you have gained along the way, principal among these being children. Another is the freedom that comes with age. It is the freedom that allows you to know and be yourself.

There is one loss that I think I will never overcome, and that is the loss of the landscape of my childhood. My relationship with nature is woven into my earliest memories, the first being the very distant image of myself seated on a branch in the elbow of a cherry tree full of white blossoms. How I came to be looking at myself in the memory—rather than out at others—is a conundrum, but there I am in the tree, peering through the blossoms at other children and far more interested in the flowers than in them. It seems to me significant now that I remember having set myself apart from the other children and that I'd already placed myself in the role of observer, including the observation of myself. The memory is vivid; the location of the tree was Monroe Township, New Jersey, near the house we'd lived in when I was born. That would have made me about three years old. So the engagement with nature was there from the beginning, and it grew as I moved through my boyhood, living an unsupervised youth made up mostly of fishing for catfish and pickerel, paying close attention to frogs and turtles, catching and examining minnows and shiners and otherwise making my own natural-history survey of central New Jersey's slow brooks and ponds.

When I was about thirteen, after a three-year interlude of urban life, which I had coped with by joining the Boy Scouts and teaching myself to fly-cast on the city grass, we moved to the Jersey shore, and it was there that I made the natural landscape my own, and brought it into my life so firmly and intimately that it became part of who I was, and who I am. It remains there today, embedded in my consciousness and sensibility, but unfortunately that is the only place where it remains, at least in the abundant way in which it once existed. The South Jersey littoral was a landscape destroyed by development, and while pockets of it remain as parks and preserves between housing tracts and marinas, the great expanse of it has disappeared. A sandy spit and scrub oak upland where I once had set up a duck blind each November to greet the lines of bluebills that would arrive from the north is now a small park with an environmental center for children. There visitors can see photos and dioramas of an ecosystem that once was rich and so common as to be taken for granted. This is true of most treasures until they are lost.

Until the beginning of the last century, the east coast of the United States was a thriving and interconnected string of bays, inlets and estuaries that were nurseries for the ocean's fishes and wintering shelters for ducks and shorebirds beyond counting. The marshes and broad mucky fields of rushes and reeds were home to mink, muskrat, raccoon, fox and deer. I remember an old Piney (as the longtime locals are known) telling the story of a swamp buck that hid in tidal lagoons during the gunning season with only his nose out of the water. The tides in these marshes rose and fell like a yogi's calm breathing and bathed the cordgrass in their gentle saline waters to feed countless tiny creatures that were the fecund foundation for a rich and mysterious web of life. My little piece of this miracle was the upper end of Barnegat Bay, a shallow stretch of fresh and salt water behind the barrier beaches that stretched from Point Pleasant to Little Egg Harbor. It was a place of cedar-stained estuaries and warm-water lagoons. The bay was inhabited by blowfish, blackfish, bluefish, striped bass, fluke, mummychogs, minnows, spearing, flounder, herring and garfish—all of which were a focus of my predatory impulses as a boy. I hunted quail and rabbits in the uplands, shot ducks from the shoreline in the fall and fished almost constantly from March through the end of October. Squeezed in there somewhere, I also dug clams and cut punks (cattails) from the bulrushes to burn as a weak mosquito repellant.

Maybe it was the age at which I encountered it—twelve going on thirteen, a time not just when a boy begins to stir sexually, but also when he begins to engage the world with an intellectual and moral consciousness—that caused this briny landscape to leave such a deep impression on me. At that age, we are trying out ideas, observing the ways in which the big world works in the little worlds we inhabit and evaluating concepts of right and wrong.

All this was happening in me as I walked through marshes, watched sunrises, swam in the brackish bay and netted crabs on sandbars.

Of course, I did not encounter this landscape in its original and pristine form. (The unspoiled Mid-Atlantic coast, in the time of the Lenni-Lenape, its bays, tidal rivers, broad marshes and the blue sea breaking on its barrier beaches, is an idea almost too beautiful to grasp.) By the time I arrived, it already was under siege, and had been for a very long time. My family was in fact part of the beginning of the final assault. Our home ("Waterfront Living, No Money Down") was in a development of modest homes going up in the piney woods and filled-in marshes as a result of the opening of the Garden State Parkway, which drew working people from the state's industrial north to its rural south. The air was cleaner, the housing cheaper.

As a boy, I saw the marshes teeming with ducks and muskrats, as well as the red surveyor flags that marked house lots and future roads. The conflict was clear. I had already developed a melancholic side, and I felt nostalgic for the natural world that preceded my birth. The sense of something being lost was already strong in me and no doubt put a darker turn on my consciousness.

I knew the men who drove the bulldozers, built the houses and sank the pilings for the docks—working-class men, many of them hard-luck cases living from paycheck to paycheck—and I was aware that they were only trying to earn a living and caught up in the machinery of something much bigger than themselves. I did not have enough experience in the world to trace back to its maleficent source the money and the mechanisms that made all this destruction possible, but I sensed that the forces that were slicing, dredging and filling the marshes were powerful, distant and not at all concerned with the fate of alligator snapper turtles, sandpipers or blue-claw crabs.

The eventual outcome was clear. It was only a matter of time. There was nothing for me to do except to spend as much time in the marshes, woods and water as possible and to acquaint myself with as much of it as I could before it was gone. And that is what I did.

When I was thirteen, fourteen and fifteen years old, I walked the curving sand and spartina of my piece of the Barnegat Bay in the early summer with a crab net, which was a five-foot broom handle at the end of which was a loop of wire and mesh net. I also carried a metal bucket that I strapped to my waist. My prey was the blue-claw crab and especially the shedder crab. The blue-claw crab increases its size by shedding its hard shell, green as rusted copper, and growing into a new and soggy parchmentlike shell. The softshell crab is a delicacy, of course. In my youth, you could buy them at bars and roadside restaurants where they were breaded and fried whole in flour and egg and served between pieces of white bread. There was a good market for softshell crabs—I could get a dollar a crab. So in June I would walk barefoot down to the bay, wearing only a pair of cutoff jeans, and wade into the water, slowly making my way through the shallows, looking on the sandy bottom or the edges of docks and bulkheads in search of the dark spots that were crabs. Catching crabs with a net took stealth and speed. At the slightest sign of danger, they skittered and swam like rockets in their sideways propulsion, or they simply dropped like stones from pilings into deep, dark water. Often at the end of a morning, though, I would have a bucket of clicking, hissing and spitting crabs, the big males defiantly waving their knuckled turquoise claws.

These tidal adventures filled my early teens. In the spring, I pursued spawning herring, shooting like silver darts into streams above the swamps and into the vast tracts of the pinelands. The cedar-stained creek water swarmed with these chromium fish. Once, camped on a swamp road in the back of a friend's wood-paneled station wagon and waiting for the sun to rise on the opening of the hunting season, I listened all through the night to the sound of lapping waves and the crank and squawk of migrating geese in the moonlit sky. In the morning, under lowering clouds, we watched rafts of ducks—thousands of ducks—skim the blue-gray chop. Some of them dropped into our wood decoys with outspread wings and lowered yellow legs. The pursuit that brought me deepest into the marshes, and closest to their secrets, was fur trapping.

I was a trapper as a boy. I caught muskrats and raccoons, skinned them in the backyard, stretched and dried their pelts on wood forms and sent the pelts off to fur buyers in New York. Today, this seems wildly anachronistic, but there was a market for wild fur in those days, and it wasn't so unusual for country boys forty or fifty years ago to earn money with a trapline. It was like having a paper route, except you got up earlier and carried a small-caliber rifle or shotgun (to shoot the occasional duck on the way home). A muskrat fetched two dollars, a raccoon three and a half. A wild mink went for upward of twenty dollars. But it wasn't the money that took me into the swamps. It was the swamps themselves that fascinated me. In late December, January and February, I got up early in the morning to make my rounds, at five a.m., well before the school bus made its grinding way down our road to pick up the children in our far-flung part of town. When I stepped from my bed, the house was quiet except for the lungs of the forced-air furnace, which blew a pleasant warmth through the grates in the floor. The windows were dark against the night. Paul was asleep in his room, my mother in hers, though I sometimes heard her stir. My mother talked in her sleep, though I could never make out what she said. If Johnny was with us, he would be with my mother or asleep on the couch, fully dressed and without a blanket. My mother was a light sleeper and aware, in a distant way, of my movement through the house. I felt it even though she didn't call out my name. The few minutes I spent getting dressed and preparing to go out into the cold and dark were a peaceful time, and I savored the anticipation of walking the route of my trapline.

I pulled on my hip waders, which I kept near the side door of the house along with my single-shot 12-gauge shotgun and a trapper's basket; I dressed in dungarees, flannel shirt, wool coat and an insulated hunter's cap with flaps that could pull down over my ears on bitter mornings; and I set off on my trapline route. I especially liked that first gulp of icy air when I stepped outside the door and felt the cold night almost immediately creep down around my neck and catch the edges of my ears. I trapped in two big marshes, one to the north on the way to Green Island, which was about a half mile from our house over two dirt roads and a patch of pine and scrub oak, and another to the south, in the direction of Snug Harbor, which took me through a more settled part of our borough.

Both marshes were a few hundred acres of muck, marsh grass,

tall reeds and tidal ponds, which were fed by cedar-stained fresh-water streams that came out of the piney woods. In those days, our little borough, which was called Silverton, renamed by developers from Mosquito Cove, still had unbroken wedges of scrub pine, oak and holly forest, made impenetrable in some places by swelling waves of briar patches, sometimes much taller than a man. Usually, the marsh would be black as ink when I reached it, but I knew its contours, paths and streams, which unfolded in the funnel of the flashlight I carried, and often—especially if the streams had frozen and the ice skim tinkled under my boots—I would startle a black duck or a mallard into flight. The marsh gave off a complicated mix of dark and musky smells that were dank and pleasant at the same time—tidal mud, rotting vegetation and swamp gas—and these odors mixed with the light tincture of the oil I had wiped my gun with the night before. It was a familiar smell, a reassuring and agreeable concoction, and it appealed to me possibly in the way that the pencil-lead-and-chalk smell of the classroom might appeal to a good student. I heard, and even felt, wing beats in the night—I was that close sometimes when the ducks exploded off the water. Their startled squawks traced their ascent. Now and again I would see them cross the light circle of the moon.

Sometimes, too, I heard ducks coming into the marsh, dropping out of the pool of black sky, especially when the great flocks were migrating south. Their wings whistled by and seemed to brush my head, though I knew the birds weren't really that close. They only seemed to be as their wings, either propelling them forward or turned down to brake them for a landing, beat the cold air into turbulence. Otherwise it would be quiet enough for me to hear them touch the water with a small splash and glide on the ponds where they set about their contented chucking. Once in a while, I heard animals that I could not see break through the marsh, splashing and snorting (maybe a deer) or scampering through the reeds (maybe a mink or a coon). Sometimes my flashlight momentarily illumined the yellow eyes of a creature that I had caught unawares as I moved quietly through the corridors of bulrushes. The eyes would blink and be gone as if the animal had made itself invisible by the action of closing its eyes.

At the center of the northern marsh, there was a hummock of cedar and sassafras, a small dry island that was surrounded by a savanna of marsh grasses the flatness of which was broken only by the rounded mounds of the muskrat lodges. If I had time, I sat there across a log, my gun in my lap, and watched the ducks gather into a line, scatter and regroup on the waters of the bay as the sky lightened from black to purple. The other, southerly marsh had a pond at its center, more accurately the widening of a stream, since the water in it flowed ever so slowly toward the bay. The bay I'm speaking of is the great Barnegat, or what was then my corner of it. The southerly marsh had a few muskrat lodges, but there the marsh blended more with the lowland and woods, a transitional place of ankle-high bushes, mossy hummocks and sassafras, and the muskrats lived mostly in dens that were dug into the banks of the stream. Some mornings I caught a muskrat or two in my traps, sometimes none at all. I had to be home before the sun rose to change into clothes for school and be ready for the bus. So all of my work was done in the dark or the magical half-light of a winter morning. Sometimes it snowed, which seemed to me a miracle. On those mornings, it was hard to leave the marsh for school.

Now even in those days, which is going on forty-five years ago, it was a little unusual for a thirteen-year-old boy to be seen walking along the road carrying a shotgun at five in the morning. Given the hour, my witnesses were few and far between, and they were mostly people forced by a long commute to be in their still-cold and sputtering Fords and Chevys, maybe to Trenton or New Brunswick. They must have lived thereabouts, because there would have been no other reason for them to be in this nook of the town. Of course, there must have been those, too, who were actually just getting home at that hour, returning from the grave-yard shift at some factory to the north or a night of local debauch and drink. I don't know and never considered it. I was submerged in my own thoughts and pleasures, happy to be warm in my clothes and feeling the straps of the pack basket on my shoulders. But people did see me, and since my trapping was no secret among my friends on the school bus, it was only natural that I developed a reputation as the boy who was a muskrat trapper. It probably added to my standing that I also caught and sold snapping turtles and shedder crabs in the summer, and I could almost always be found in the months of July and August on the bay fishing for blackfish, blues or fluke.

All of which is to say it should have come to me as no surprise when one day a neighbor told me that there was a man who lived near the swamp, the one on the way to Green Island, who wanted me to come by for a job. She described him as an older man who had recently moved down from "the city," which is the way nearly everyone there referred to North Jersey. This was in the summer, July, in the best part of the gardening season, when the lettuces were coming up in big green leaves in the dark sandy soil and under the hot Jersey sun. The man had gotten my name while sitting in Silverton's only tavern, Toby's. The owner of the bar, Toby, was a malevolent character. The bar had made him prosperous—he owned a new Buick and traveled to Florida for a few weeks in the winter. He also owned hunting dogs, mostly rabbit hounds, and had a reputation for cruel training methods. If a dog didn't meet his standards, it was cast off or shot. Johnny drank there, and sometimes he brought me inside the bar. I sat on a bar stool with him and drank birch beer. Toby let Johnny run a tab, and this appeared to give him power over Johnny. He was deferential to Toby in a way I had not seen him with anyone else. I owned one of Toby's cast-off dogs, a gun-shy English Pointer named Joe. Toby's bar opened in the morning for men who couldn't wait until noon for a drink and was a place to drop off and pick up information—the availability of part-time work, local squabbles, where fish were being caught and the like. One day the man who had moved to the place near the swamp had come into Toby's and complained over his beer that the muskrats were cleaning out his garden. Toby told him that he knew a boy who could rid him of the muskrats. My neighbor's husband had been present for the exchange, and she related it to me. "He will pay you," she said.

It was July, certainly not trapping season. Motivated less by lucre and more by ego and the flattery of having had my name spoken in Toby's as a trapper, I knocked on the man's door. It was a sweltering day—nothing like my winter mornings in the swamp. He was a small dark man, and a television was mumbling somewhere in the house. He came out and took me to his garden. He showed me the garden damage and offered me a price. I came back the next day with a half dozen traps, and over the next days began catching the muskrats that were slipping into his garden at night. The man was pleased. "You really know how to catch those bastards," he said. But each day as I stood in the summer sun I felt worse and worse about taking the dead muskrats from the traps—the pelts of the muskrats I was catching were useless in summer. They lacked the deep loft of fur and the black-and-brown sheen of the animals I caught in the winter. And there was nothing to do with the carcasses, so I buried them in a corner of his garden.

This trapping brought me none of the pleasure that I got from my winter rounds in the marsh. It seemed more than a waste; what I was doing seemed a sacrilege. I even stopped lifting my eyes to the marsh when I was in the man's garden. I felt ashamed. On about the fourth day, I gathered up my traps, and without saying a word to the man, I walked away from his house with no intention of going back. I didn't ask for the money I was owed. The money would have made me feel even worse. A couple of weeks after I had put the episode out of my mind, my neighbor told me the man with the garden was awfully pleased with the work I had done since the muskrats were no longer eating his garden. "He wants to pay you," she said. I went back to feeling bad and that winter didn't return to the marsh as a trapper. I had done something terribly wrong, and I was sure the marsh was aware of it, and if it wasn't, I surely was.

This memory—of killing muskrats out of season so a man who had a summer house down the shore could put his garden too close to a marsh—remained buried for forty years. An essay by

Václav Havel brought it back to mind, and in reading it I reexperienced the disappointment in myself for having agreed to eliminate those creatures for money.

In the essay, "Politics and Conscience," Havel remembers a disturbing sight from his boyhood, of a factory smokestack polluting the sky:

> Each time I saw it, I had an intense sense of something profoundly wrong, of humans soiling the heavens. I have no idea whether there was something like a science of ecology in those days; if there was, I certainly knew nothing of it. Still that "soiling of the heavens" offended me spontaneously. It seemed to me that, in it, humans are guilty of something, that they destroy something important, arbitrarily disrupting the natural order of things, and that such things cannot go unpunished. To be sure, my revulsion was largely aesthetic; I knew nothing then of the noxious emissions which would one day devastate our forests, exterminate game, and endanger the health of people.

Havel speculates that a medieval peasant would have had the same reaction as he, a boy—a shared intuition of something terribly wrong, of some natural, higher law being violated.

> What is it, actually, that the world of the medieval peasant and that of a small boy have in common? Something substantive, I think. Both the boy and the peasant are far more intensely rooted in what some philosophers call "the natural world," or *Lebenswelt*, than most modern adults. They have not yet grown alienated from the world of their actual personal experience, the

world which has its morning and its evening, its down (the earth) and its up (the heavens), where the sun rises daily in the east, traverses the sky and sets in the west, and where concepts like "at home" and "in foreign parts," good and evil, beauty and ugliness, near and far, duty and rights, still mean something living and definite. They are still rooted in a world which knows the dividing line between all that is intimately familiar and appropriately a subject of our concern, and that which lies beyond its horizon, that before which we should bow down humbly because of the mystery about it.

Few boys now are trappers, and most of us live in cities. Technology has separated us from farms, fields and woods. So the question that nags me is this: Has the departure of nature from our lives impaired our ability to make moral decisions? And by extension, does this account for the way we treat the earth?

CHAPTER 4

FOUNDATION

Our immediate objective on the hillside was sixteen holes, five feet deep and eighteen inches across. Into each hole, we would place a heavy-duty cardboard tube twelve inches in diameter, then surround it with dirt to ground level before filling it with wet concrete to the grade of the cabin. The concrete would dry into hard permanent piers that would reach below the frost line of the hillside's soil. Such was the plan to create the foundation.

It was a marvelous conception, so easily executed in the abstract.

I rented a small backhoe from a tool and equipment store outside of Portland the night before the work was to begin, and we drove up to the cabin with it on a trailer behind Paul's truck. We spent the night at a nearby inn that was a vestige of the old ski area—a long articulated building with two levels of simple and inexpensive rooms and a center lodgelike space at the knuckle with a big fireplace. We wanted to get an early start. Our room had a kitchenette, Murphy bed and pullout couch. Paul crashed on the couch without pulling out its bed, the back of his head resting against one arm of the couch and his legs slung over the other arm. He had always been able to sleep anywhere with ease. I remember him once as a teenager, after a three-day disappearance, putting down an unbroken thirty-six-hour sleep on the living room carpet. My brother was no insomniac. I asked him if he wanted to share the Murphy bed, and he was already asleep. That night he had not seemed in the mood to talk anyway. I put a blanket over him. I read for a while, then dozed off.

In the morning, Paul climbed onto the backhoe and started the engine. It fired up with loud popping sounds as if firecrackers had been dropped into the upright exhaust pipe. It roared when he put it into gear and moved it to the position of the first hole. But then he shut it down, got off the machine and handed me the key.

"Go for it," he said.

Me?

I was not ready for this. There was a subtle shift in the hierarchy of the work, or workers. I thought he would dig the holes. He was better at this work. The man on the backhoe was going to be the one shouldering the work for the day. I had just assumed he would operate the backhoe and I would assist with a shovel. No, he was handing the project back to me. Was he telling me that he would help with this project but he wasn't going to let me, slyly as the smart big brother, set it down on him? Or was the message, maybe unconsciously, even more profound? Was he telling me to give up on the role of older and more sensitive brother, which insinuated him into his old childhood role of bad and irresponsible boy, and to recognize him as an adult? In other words, was he telling me to acknowledge that he had grown up? I looked into his eyes, and I could see that he wasn't climbing onto the backhoe.

I climbed up to the seat, started the engine and tried out the hydraulic levers that moved the bucket up and down and right and left. They jerked madly like some spasmodic insect, and I was unable to get the smooth swing of a professional operator. I dropped the teeth of the bucket into the ground and opened the first hole, on the front left side of the cabin, under what eventually would be the porch. Paul set about lining up grade stakes and strings and marking the positions of each of the holes with a can of red spray paint. He was doing the brain work; I was doing the grunt work.

There is no month in Maine worse for work than November. It is the rainy season, and the rain mixes with below-freezing temperatures to make sleet, slush and frozen mud. Even the loggers wait until December before they take their equipment into the woods. The day was cold and overcast, but so far we were lucky—it had not yet snowed, and we felt only the occasional bit of drizzle through the day. Now and again, I heard the report of a rifle in the distance. It was the last Saturday of the deer season.

The hardest part of the backhoe work was dropping the dirt that came out of the holes in the right place and moving the machine from hole to hole. All the digging was inside the footprint of the cabin, and I was fast running out of room. It was difficult to both pile the dirt and keep enough space open for the machine to change its position for the next hole. To make matters worse, I was making no progress on smoothing the swing of the bucket. Occasionally, a bucket spasm knocked dirt back onto the hole I had just dug. I had to start over. I began to wish that I had insisted on the auger. It would have yielded sixteen clean and easily dug holes. Who cared if one was off a bit? I should have stood my ground against Paul's objection. I sat on the backhoe, fumbled with the controls and nursed my failure to insist on the auger approach. I held my anger and stayed silent.

A more serious problem soon developed. Water began to collect at the bottom of the holes I was digging, lots of water, and it began oozing into the holes at just two feet of depth. We were contending with a seriously shallow water table. Given the altitude of the cabin and the positive drainage down the hillside, this took me by surprise. It was as if we were trying to dig holes at the beach. The sides of some of the wettest holes began to collapse, and pretty soon they were three feet across and full of mud and water. The wider holes made it even more difficult to move the machine. The job was fast becoming hopeless.

Our water problem had a long history. The great Laurentide glacier had crept down from the north about ninety thousand years ago and covered the northern tier of what is now the United States. Thousands of feet thick and enormously heavy, the burden of its weight depressed the surface of the earth. Ice reached from the Pacific to the Atlantic oceans, and in the east as far out as Georges Bank. Eventually, as the earth's climate warmed a few degrees, the monster glacier began to retreat and, about twelve thousand years ago, melted its way out of Maine. In its exit, water flowed from the glacier's base and spread sediment of varying textures, from fine clay to bony gravel, over the landscape. The result was a kind of geologic layer cake of soils that rested atop the earth's crust. The hillside was a good representation of the layer cake. Its bottom layer was a fine dense clay, the next layer was sand and gravel, and the shallow top layer, which began to form after the glacier's departure and while giant mammals still roamed the region, was a mat of organic material, black soil made from the decomposition of the forest and webbed together with the roots of small plants. The layer cake was strewn with big rocks that floated freely in the clay and gravel. These rocks had been scraped from the earth's crust to the north and carried south by the wall of ice during its advance and then held in its belly until it began its crawl back to the north. In its retreat, the glacier dropped its rocky baggage here, around my cabin site, and of course, the rest of New England. Those rocks had then slept deep in the ground for millennia, but once the land had been cleared of its trees and cultivated by the first European settlers, frost was able to reach farther down into the ground, and slowly the freezing and thawing of moisture in the soil worked the stones to the surface. The early farmers found themselves with a new crop of stones each year. They lifted them from the fronts of their plows and piled them into stone walls. The stones are still working their way up and out of the ground as any New England gardener knows.

A close look at the mountains to the north and west of the cabin elaborates on the glacier's story. The northern slopes of the mountains are relatively smooth. The ice sheet simply rode up and over them as it moved along. But the opposite, southerly slopes are ragged and sometimes sheered off. The ice sheet had grabbed these leeward slopes in its frozen underside and ripped off the faces as it inched forward, grinding the bare rock into pebbles. The contours of the land around about the cabin could nearly all be explained by the descent and retreat of the giant ice sheet.

At the cabin site, what was happening as I dug the holes was this: the water that had fallen on the hillside through the fall and summer had collected in the soil and percolated into the gravel. Some of it stayed there; some of it ran down the slope over the smooth dense surface of the clay. There had been plenty of rain, of course, so the hillside was saturated like sponge. When we opened the holes, we gave all that water in the gravel a place to run to and collect. Each hole had become an inground cistern, a muddy, sloppy mess of gravel, clay and soupy water.

There was no way we could set cardboard tubes into the holes. In an hour, the paper would be as limp as a wet slice of bread. So here on the first day of construction, we had a big problem. For builders, there is no problem like a water problem. I watched the holes fill with water and wondered when I would get cut a break. There had been the driveway problem, the ledge problem, the rain problem, the excavator problem and now the water table problem.

We talked it over. Paul suggested we come back with a mud-sucking pump, a device that is half gasoline engine, half lamprey eel, to empty the holes of water and substitute precast piers for the cardboard tubes. We would forego pouring the concrete ourselves. The precast piers would not reach below the frost line since they were only four feet long and needed to extend at least a foot out of the ground, and sometimes more where the grade of the ground declined, but we saw no alternative. Paul thought we also needed a load of stone delivered to the site to firm up the muddy bottoms of the holes. I concurred and silently did the math on the mounting cost of the foundation. I would have to rent the pump, buy the precast piers and the stone and pay the trucking charge to get it to the site. We called it a day as a half dozen luckless hunters fired their guns into the air to mark sunset and the end of the deer season, without having shot a deer. It seemed an appropriately futile salute to a miserable day.

The next weekend we returned with reinforcements. In addition to renting the backhoe again, Paul's three sons joined us: Paulie, Kevin, a mason who had been laid off from his job, and Andrew, the oldest son and recently back from Iraq, where he had served as a corpsman in a marine combat unit. They were strong young men and good workers. Well, maybe Paulie did more joshing and joking than working, but he was good company. I was elated to have them with me.

The holes were full of water, clear at the top and muddy at the bottom, with icy rims. To make matters worse, it had rained and then snowed just enough during the week to cover the ground and make it slick. The ground was frozen to a depth of a couple inches. Paul started the pump and dropped the big hose into the water. Andrew climbed on the backhoe. He was far more adept at swinging the bucket than I and began cleaning the old holes and digging new ones. Kevin helped Andrew from the ground, using a shovel inside the holes to clear mud and straighten the walls. Wearing boots, he climbed down into the water, scooped the mud and lifted it out. It was cold and dirty work, but he went at it with enthusiasm. He paused only to goad Paulie, who was building a fire to stay warm and playing with his dog, Koda. "Hey, Paulie," Kevin hollered over the roar of the pump. "Don't strain yourself over there while the rest of us are working." I pushed wheelbarrow loads of stone and poured them into the holes. Kevin climbed out of the hole each time and filled the wheelbarrow from the pile at the top of the driveway. In no time, Koda got tangled in the foundation lines Paul had set, and in his struggle pulled up two of the grade stakes. "For Chrissake, Paulie, get a hold on that dog!" Kevin shouted. I was prepared to shoot the dog. Fortunately for Koda, I was unarmed. Paulie chased Koda down and leashed him to a tree, where he spent the next hour barking disconsolately at nothing in particular. We worked furiously into the afternoon, barely making progress against the constant flow of water. The pump was sucking, gorging on muddy water and spewing it through a pipe about twenty yards from the cabin site. We paused around one o'clock, and over the campfire heated a big tin of rigatoni Paul had cooked the night before and had brought along. We considered the situation. The rigatoni disappeared quickly but the situation did not improve with discussion. We had worked like mules and set only four of the sixteen piers. It was now two p.m., and the sun was just over the treetops and soon to be behind the mountain. It was December 6. Tomorrow would be colder than today, and the day after that colder still. The days were getting shorter. Soon the ground would freeze too deep for the small backhoe to break it. We knocked off at sunset, discouraged and silent.

I decided to call my reliable but expensive driveway excavator. He counseled sanity: wait until spring. I was unwilling. The start of the cabin had lifted my spirits; the work was taking me outside into the cold air, and I enjoyed my trips to Stoneham, even when I went alone and even when things didn't go perfectly. This was why I wanted a cabin, to be outdoors and working with my brother and nephews, and all of that argued against suspending the work. Even if we stopped, I would still be up there walking in the woods and puttering around at the cabin site. I might as well be working on the cabin.

None of this made any sense to him, I think, and he asked what exactly it was I wanted him to do. I said I wanted him to dig twelve holes in the frozen ground and clean out four others while I pumped them dry enough to set down the precast piers. He more or less said, "Okay, it's your money." He charged $150 an hour for his big machine, and he would hire a man to come along at $25 an hour. I was looking at close to $1,500 to keep the project moving. I swallowed hard and said yes.

Kevin joined me the following Saturday. The excavator was there with his man, so that made four of us. The machine cracked the icy earth as if it were nothing more than crust on a burnt casserole, and the three of us on the ground set the concrete piers in the new holes and backfilled them with stone and clods of frozen soil. The excavator cleaned the existing holes of mud and we planted piers in them too. It sleeted the entire day, and at times poured down a heavy rain. We worked in rubber slickers and high boots. Kevin's ungloved hands were wet, red and cold. He maintained a cheerful attitude and kept working even when I went to get all of us lunch and hot coffee at the Center Lovell Market. We stayed with it until dark, and by then we had all of the piers in the ground.

I took a deep breath. The foundation was in.

The top of the piers defined my work surface at two feet above the little bit of snow that covered the ground. So, unless a big storm blew through the hills, which was more than just a possibility, I knew I would be able to move rapidly to the next step, which was to set the girders on the piers and frame the floor. It was winter, but in this race to erect the cabin, I was leading by a neck. Paul said he was unavailable for the next few weeks, and I had student papers to mark up and grades to submit anyway. Work ceased. I watched the forecast for snow. It came down, an inch or two at a time almost every night, and soon it was more than a foot deep, but it remained below the tops of those piers.

In the two-week pause, I made a trip to the site to look things over and stroll the hillside and surrounding woods. I had been walking alone in the winter woods my entire life and never found them without surprise, joy or inspiration. I put on my snowshoes and made my way over the undisturbed snow to the cabin site and then pushed higher up the hillside, pausing among the stand of red pines, allowing myself to think again that this would make a good place for an orchard; then I moved farther to the top of the ridge, which gave me a view of Adams Mountain, brown and gray against the scudding clouds. I turned downhill on an old logging road that followed an ancient stone wall. The experience of the woods in winter is almost entirely visual: shadow and sunlight; tree trunks black, gray and white, some of them smooth as suede, others rough as oyster shells. The light is everything, turning ice-tipped branches into ornaments and the quartz caught in granite boulders into pink jewels. I stopped from time to time to absorb the silence. The winter woods are nearly always silent. There may be the muffled woof of snow falling from the burdened bough of a spruce tree or the isolated chatter of chickadees as they search among the softwood for seeds, but usually the only sound is the rasp of one's own breathing. I walked for an hour, letting my mind empty itself into the frozen landscape.

Walking was one of the ways I marshaled my feelings and thoughts and brought my mind and body together into a union of well-being. I often take long walks to settle questions, quiet my mind or warm and regulate my muscles and breathing. If I find myself in a new city, I often walk well into the night down unknown streets to distant landmarks and near exhaustion. It sharpens my senses and brings me to a state of greater awareness of myself and my surroundings. At home in Boston, if my mind is a swarm of bees or if I am absorbing the power of some book I have just finished reading, I go to the streets and begin walking. Each step brings me closer to a feeling of clear comprehension and a sense of both pleasantly inhabiting but not being limited by my body. Maybe this was what the Greeks were aiming at when they spoke of *eudaimonia,* the sense of well-being that is the aspiration of right thinking. Walking was also part of cabin building, and there was no better walk than a walk in the woods.

It was always a wonder to me how quickly the woods returned me to a sense of beginning again—of a fresh start. It had always been this way with me. Walking an old woods trail and breathing cold air or sitting on a fallen tree trunk to watch an owl surveil the frozen woods for prey—these are talismanic experiences. Nature offers a direct and uncomplicated relationship to the world. It is free of the distorting complications of ambition, shame, disappointment or pride—all of which pollute the joy and beauty that is so freely given by nature.

Here in the woods, there was no spin, and nothing was false or insincere. Is it a coincidence that truth seems in short supply in those places that are bereft of nature? I wanted to tear sham and pretense from my throat—to rip out all the lies—and if that meant pulling out adhering flesh, that would be all right too. What would be left would be clean and honest. I turned back to the cabin, making a circle rather than retracing my steps. By the time I got back, the sun was about to set.

I was struck by the short arc the sun had traveled through the course of the day. I smiled: it had been a short transit for both of us. The sun had risen on the far side of the pond and now it was setting between the near side of the pond and Adams Mountain. If the circle of the horizon roundabout the cabin had been the face of a clock, with north at noon, the sun would have risen in the morning at the four o'clock position and set in the evening at the seven o'clock position—not much of a trip at all. It had been in the sky only eight and a half hours. Back in May, it would have risen around the two o'clock position and set at the eight o'clock position and spent thirteen and a half hours in the sky. The pinched arc did more than shorten the days. The winter tilt of the earth also kept the sun low in the sky. It was this low route and the trajectory of its light that flattened the ground late in the day. The pale sunlight had skimmed over the surface of this little piece of earth and had given the trees long shadows. Now even those long shadows were disappearing in the dusk. A little wind stirred in the cold air, but I stayed seated on the pile of lumber I had cleared of its pillow of snow. I could sit there all night, I thought.

The light was seeping from the woods, and the dark spaces among the trees were utterly silent. This had always been a sacred part of the day for me. The light was dying, and soon it would be night, a bright winter night. The night sky in winter is a marvelous thing. It gives capacity to the mind and dimension for thought and ideas and provides the clarity necessary to see the world as it is, and not as it has been delivered to us by the peddlers of cant and convention, which is nearly always a way of keeping us from our true selves. I sat there, pulled my light coat up to my chin and remembered back to my earlier life, the one in which I was the father of two young children. There had been a night, a powerfully cold night, as I recall, much colder than this one, and for some reason I had been drawn to go outside of the house to look at the stars. The house had been complete for five or six years by then, and my wife and I and our children were well settled into it. The night had been moonless and clear, and there was a profusion of stars. I found the North Star and turned in place to take in the entire sky. It had been a night in which the stars actually sparkled; they glittered, it seemed, for my benefit. The snow was deep and creaked under my boots. The temperature was well below zero and a pale wraith of smoke drifted up from the chimney as the woodstove inside pulsed with heat. I had stood there for a very long time, letting the cold find its way into my woolen shirt, and I thought I would never be happier.

In the week before Christmas, I drove to Paul's house for the night to break up the drive to the cabin. Now, with his house emptying itself of children as they grew up and moved out, he always had a spare bedroom for me. I slept in one of his girls' rooms, with high school photos and posters of boy movie stars on the walls, and woke early. Andrew was still on leave, and he said he would join me for the day's work. I knocked on his bedroom door at six a.m., and together we loaded Paul's truck with tools and a generator for powering a saw. The sun was rising and it was cold—fourteen degrees in Portland. No doubt it was colder in the hills. Paul could not join us, but he was letting me use his truck; I left my car for him. Andrew called Kevin, who lived downtown with his girl-friend and her mother, to see if he wanted to come along for the day's work. I hit the jackpot: Kevin said yes, and both one of his friends and Paulie wanted to come along too. That would make five of us to frame the floor. It gave me a good shot at getting it done.

I was especially glad to have Kevin along. He had demon-strated his willingness to work during the foundation fiasco. But I also saw in him an uncanny strategic sense. He liked to plan a job. He shared this trait with his father: he had a very well-developed sense of spatial relationships, and he was always look-ing ahead to the next step and around the corner for a hidden problem. Except that Kevin would look ahead three or four steps. He would say something like this: "You know, Uncle Louie, I think if we put this there first, and then follow it with that, we can avoid having to carry that as far, and we will be able to just lift that over there with a lot less effort." Huh? I was astonished at these insights, and they proved more and more useful as the cabin took shape.

I also liked to have him with me because his mind was con-stantly turning things over. He chattered through the day about this and that—interesting programs he had seen on Animal Planet or the Discovery Channel, newspaper stories reporting govern-ment waste, as well as a stream of personal observations on the world's ineptitude. The list was long: taxes, war, the prices of vari-ous products at the supermarket, certain motor vehicle laws, peo-ple who cut in line, pet owners who didn't walk their dogs often enough, inaccurate weather forecasts, the cost of meals at some restaurants, global warming. He was constantly evaluating the scene around him and trying to fit the pieces together. The process seemed to require that he put all of his incipient thoughts into spoken language. I was his audience as we worked.

Kevin's life had had a rough beginning. Less than twelve hours after his birth, a nurse noticed he was spitting up dark bile. She alerted the doctor, who quickly diagnosed the cause: his large intestine had ruptured. The doctor took Paul aside: "I can remove the ruptured intestine, but I don't know if he can survive the operation. Without it, I'm certain he will die. The decision on what to do is yours." Paul's response: "There is no choice. Operate." The doctor removed Kevin's large intestine and some of his small intestine, and he spent the next six months in the hospital.

It was during this period that I had in a sense betrayed Paul. I had not gone to see Kevin in the hospital then and was only remotely aware at the time of the problems Kevin and Paul were facing. My mother, who had moved to Portland to be near her sons, was the intermediary. I was absorbed in my job and my own life and was seeing Paul only intermittently. Life was going well for me then: my children were young and happy, my marriage seemed to be sound and I was busy and rising fast at the newspaper. I was beginning to accumulate a few extra dollars. Paul was in Portland working construction at the time and coping with a very sick child. I should have been there at his side, but I was not. It was a failure I could not take back. This period of disconnection between us lasted nearly five years, the time during which Paul's other children were born. One day, when we were alone and driving back from work at the cabin and talking about Kevin, I apologized to Paul for not coming through for him. It was a painful moment and I was not eager to explore my failure—I just wanted to get it off my chest and apologize.

"I should have been there for you then, and I wasn't," I said. "I'm sorry."

"Don't worry about it," Paul said. "I don't even remember."

I think he did remember. He was giving me a pass.

Kevin was Paul's second child and encountered the problems typical of a middle child—he'd felt that his older and younger brothers got more attention from his father, and that his two sisters got more attention than all of them. To confound the problem, turning it from something not unusual into something more troubling, Kevin had gone to live with his mother after Paul and she had broken up. He was about ten at the time, and the separation from his siblings increased his perception of being left out. He was a sensitive boy, aware of everyone's feelings—sometimes more than his own—and he felt overlooked. Occasionally he brooded on the unfairness of it. Eventually, he moved back with Paul and his brothers and sisters, and a kind of unity was restored. But he carried an angry flame inside. Sometimes that anger surfaced with too much drinking, and when he drank he inevitably got into trouble. Kevin, who was otherwise bright and often intensely logical, had a way of putting himself exactly in the wrong place at the wrong time—like on one night of July Fourth fireworks when he got into a fight with a group of boys and ended up hitting a Portland policeman who was trying to break it up. It was assault on a police officer, and it landed him in jail. More recently, with counseling and honest self-appraisal, he had worked through his anger and was showing a more grown-up self. He had gotten a job as a mason; he liked the work, excelled at it and, though he'd recently been laid off, intended to return to it. In our long afternoon talks, I suggested he might want to open his own masonry business. His father and I would help him get started, I said.

Andrew, of course, was now a hero in the family. He had served two tours of duty in Iraq as a navy corpsman assigned to a marine combat unit. In his first deployment to Iraq, in 2006, he served with the 1st Battalion, 9th Marines in Diyala Province; in his second deployment, in 2007, he served with the 3rd Battalion, 6th Marines in Anbar Province. His job on both tours was emergency medicine in combat. Andrew had always set himself apart as an individual and a bit of a loner—he was an outstanding long-distance runner, and (I'm willing to bet) one of the best deer hunters in the state of Maine. You could hardly put him in the woods when he was growing up without him finding and shooting a deer. He moved through the woods as quietly as smoke. After high school, he enrolled in a vocational school to study boat building and engine repair, and went to work at a marina in South Portland. He grew bored with the work and joined the navy to shake up his life, which he did with distinction. He had been recognized with leadership awards through his period of training and had made it a point of personal pride to attain an elite level of physical fitness. He defeated his marine brothers in push-up contests. In Iraq, he had experienced combat and had been thrown from a Humvee by a roadside explosive device.

At the hillside, I put Paul's truck into four-wheel drive and took it partway up the driveway, which was covered with snow. Below the snow there was ice. The five of us shuffled through the powder from the truck to the cabin and hauled the generator with us. The sky was mostly blue with a few drifting gray clouds. It was cold and dry, a good day to work.

The battle plan was to first build four girders that would span the length of the cabin and rest on the concrete piers. The boys stood ready and awaited my directions. I explained the tasks, the materials and the sequence of construction. Of course Kevin had suggestions on how to arrange the materials to lay up the girders more efficiently. I took his suggestions and we pushed forward, each with our own duties. Andrew pulled the two-by-eights from under the tarp and snow. Kevin's friend followed and soon we were working together smoothly as a team. Paulie built a fire and moved between it and the work. We matched, staggered and nailed the two-by-eights together to form the girders, and then lifted each into place atop the concrete pillars. Soon we were marking and cutting the joists and installing the joist hangers to the girders. We slipped the joists into place, forming a latticework that looked like the inside of a piano.

The floor of the main part of the cabin, the long rectangle, was fully framed by about four p.m., and a cold winter dusk settled over our work. The sun was behind the trees, and dark blue-black streaks formed in the sky. We had only the floor frame of the ell left to complete. It was a very respectable day's work, and I was satisfied with our achievement.

"Shall we call it a day, boys?" I asked. "We got a lot done."

"No," Kevin immediately said. "Let's get it all done. I say we finish it."

I looked to the others, and they shrugged in agreement, carried away by Kevin's enthusiasm.

I admired our work in the dying light and praised my crew. "Son of a bitch if it doesn't look like a cabin is going up," I said.

On the way home, Paulie, Kevin and his friend fell asleep in the backseat of the truck. Andrew rode with me in the front, and we talked of this and that. He missed Maine, he said, and he was eager to get home. He was counting the days until his discharge. Too much bullshit in the military, he said. He had declined an offer of more money to reenlist for a third tour in Iraq. His plans were vague: maybe he would use his emergency medical training as a civilian; maybe he would start a business.

"I think I'd like to build a cabin too someday," he said. "When I get the money."

"We can do that," I said, pleased he was drawn to the project. "We can practice on this one and build yours right."

Two weeks later, after Christmas, Kevin, Paulie and I returned and put plywood over the girders and joists to make a deck, which would be the cabin's subfloor. Paul said he was having trouble getting away—commitments at home and the church again. My nephews hauled the plywood up the hillside with a sled and snow-mobile, and together we nailed the four-by-eight-foot sheets into place, using countless handfuls of nails, each of which required about four strokes of the heavy framing hammer. The hammer blows resounded in the frozen woods. By the end of December, my shoulder was sore and my right forearm was a knot, but we had a platform, something to walk on. The snow was getting deeper, but my work surface had risen too. The race was tightening. Now we were moving into the deeper and colder part of winter. My lead had diminished to a nose.

The next step would be the one I enjoyed the most: building the timber frame. It would be Kevin and I together, getting it done as a two-man team.

CHAPTER 5

BROTHERS

One day while I was working on the hillside, it occurred to me that the cabin, in a way, would be the embodiment of our mutual biographies, Paul's and mine, blended into a single 640-square-foot structure sitting on concrete piers. Here we were, two brothers who had managed to remain close despite the passage of years and periods of separation. We had the same parents, had grown up in the same household, eaten the same food and drunk the same water, yet we had different temperaments and sensibilities. Outwardly we had led different lives, but inwardly we had similar values and impulses, which had come out of our strong shared experiences as children and young men: blood loyalty and the resourcefulness that children learn from having to wash out their underwear and socks in the bathroom sink each night before school or lift an alcoholic stepfather out of the bushes and clean him up in the house. All of this, the similarities and the differences, was playing out, and would further play out, as the cabin took its shape.

My mother often had made the observation that I was the

good boy, Paul the bad boy. I heard it a hundred times: "Paul, you're so bad!" For many years, I believed it. Looking back, I see that it's enough to make a child psychiatrist shudder. Many years had to pass before I saw the inaccuracy and unfairness of it.

A story my mother repeated over and over again was about the time Paul, at age five, had deliberately gotten himself lost at the Korvettes department store in East Brunswick, New Jersey, so he could hear his name called over the public address system. "Shoppers, we have a lost boy in the office. His name is Paul. Will his family please come to the office at the rear of the store?" My mother was pushing dresses on hangers up and down the rack to find something that would fit when she heard her son's name. She looked around. There was no Paul. She knew immediately that it was her Paul at the office. Her reaction was not worry. The announcement of the lost child was affirmation of her view that Paul just wanted to make a little excitement for himself or stir up some trouble whenever possible. We retrieved him. There he was, savoring his fame, attended by the store's female assistant manager among piles of clothes, bare hangers and empty coffee cups in the tiny office. Paul was physically small then, even for his age, with blue-gray eyes, light brown hair and an impish grin. He greeted us sitting down. "You're so bad!" my mother said as she grabbed him by the hand and led us both back to the dress rack, somewhere between sizes 16 and 18. It was only much later that I understood that she had secretly loved him for his unruliness. She admired rebellion. Maybe it was one of the reasons our family was always on the wrong side of authority and, indirectly, why we were always broke and on the move.

My earliest memory of Paul was the time the robbers held up

our stagecoach at Cowboy City. I could not have been more than seven years old, because my father is in the memory. Paul would have been three or four. Our mother and father—a memorable event in itself, that they were together—had taken Paul and me to Cowboy City, a low-budget theme park near our home in central New Jersey. There was a saloon, general store, wood-plank sidewalk and sheriff's office with a jail. Cowboys with chaps and guns on their hips swaggered around the little town. They came flying out of the saloon and were dragged into jail by the sheriff and his deputies. In their big boots and spurs, they seemed seven feet tall. There was a stagecoach ride, which we took, and at the edge of town the coach was stopped by a group of cowboys on horseback wearing neckerchiefs over their faces and firing their guns into the air. The horses spun around and made a big cloud of dust.

The cowboys ordered all of us out of the coach. It was a holdup. They demanded the chest from the driver. I had not been let in on the joke, and to me all this was as real as a traffic accident. When one of the cowboys approached us, to heighten the drama, I stepped forward and said something like, "Leave us alone. We weren't bothering you." Of course, the cowboy thought this was funny. My eyes must have flashed, or maybe they had filled with tears. I stood my ground and held Paul by the hand close to me. "Don't you hurt my brother," I warned the cowboy. The cowboy stopped laughing, and so did the adults who had been on the stagecoach enjoying this little bit of theater. I was dead serious, and while I was unarmed, I was prepared to do whatever it took to defend my brother and me.

My mother loved to tell this story, too, because it contained the elements of character that she honored most: resistance, courage and fealty to blood. Somehow lost in her retellings of the story were the points that I was scared out of my wits and that I hadn't turned to the adults around me for protection. I may have wet the cowboy pants I was wearing for the day, the ones with fringes down the legs—not the last time my bladder let loose in a childhood full of close calls, real and imagined. For a long time, the Cowboy City story was the perfect emblem of the relationship between Paul and me.

It is difficult enough for any of us to unsplice the strands of our separate identities as individuals; it is even more difficult to understand the nature of a relationship, which possesses its own identity and shapes the behavior of the people inside it through a complicated reverb of expectations, perceptions and emotional history. I think there is still something of the Cowboy City dynamic acting between Paul and me, though much has changed.

I'm also guessing that Paul and I together are not exactly the same people we are apart. Together, we behave in ways that tap into the demands and consequences of our history. I think this is probably not unusual. It seems to me unlikely that any person has one true self. We have an array of tightly packed contingencies of self, which may differ in small and not necessarily hypocritical ways, and we shuffle among them depending on the present moment and the force field of our relationships. Sometimes Paul and I need a break from each other's company, to breathe the air outside of brotherhood, but I'm also guessing that we are, more often than not, our better selves when we are together, especially when we are working.

Paul comes in and out of my childhood memories like a cat in a quiet room. Sometimes he's there; sometimes he's not. I must have been watching out for myself most of the time as we were growing up and working out the confusion and trouble that was almost always going on around me—the shouting, the drinking, the insecurity. I also sensed from an early age that Paul's only real vulnerability was his size and that if he ever grew big he would be able to handle the world better than I ever could. How did I understand this at age seven? I don't know, but I did.

The good-boy epithet that my mother hung on me could not have been entirely true, even though she had me convinced of it. Paul was a stutterer as a child. (Occasionally, he still halts for the briefest moment at a word when he's making an explanation. No one is aware of it except for me, I think.) His stuttering was getting worse when he was about eight, and somehow the school nurse got involved. There was a conference with my mother at Lee Street Elementary School in New Brunswick, where we lived for just over three years in the same apartment, a long stretch for us. There was a series of follow-ups with a woman who was (I'm guessing) a speech pathologist. I recall her wearing a white uniform and white stockings, and those meetings and examinations concluded with the speech pathologist suggesting that I—the good boy!—was part of the problem. She wanted me to stop correcting Paul when he spoke.

"You must try not to interrupt him, or tell him what he's doing wrong," she said.

So I guess I must have been a bit of a shit when I was eleven or twelve, already a little too perfect. I remember, too, that we used to fight a lot—real fights, wrestling on the ground, rubbing knuckles in the scalp, headlocks. I was bigger and always won the fights, though there may have been a few that ended in a deadlock because Paul was unwilling to admit defeat. The source of the fights was almost always my attempt to coerce him into helping me clean the house, or some small part of it. My mother worked at her hairdresser job six days a week and was content with a messy home, and I often felt compelled to straighten it out for her. My compulsion was not so strong that I was willing to do it by myself. Each of our housecleaning sessions thus was usually preceded by a half hour of tussling. I would get up from watching after-school television and tell Paul we had to clean up before Mom got home, and he would say no. To get his cooperation, sometimes it was enough to push Paul's arm up behind his back in a chicken wing to the point of pain; other times stronger measures were required to get him to clear and wipe the kitchen table. Paul, by the way, disputes all of this, claiming it was he who wanted to clean the house and I who refused. This is absolutely not true. He claims the fights were over my demand that he scratch my back. Again, completely not true. We took turns scratching each other's backs, and I always gave him exactly the same number of minutes of scratching time that he gave me.

As we grew up, Paul was always more popular and social than I. He kept count of his friends and could tell the number he had down to the person. He would occasionally brag that he had eleven or eighteen or twenty-three friends. He wrote down their names. He spent his time with them, playing, and later carousing, and was usually away most of the day from whatever house or apartment we were living in. He went out for sports teams and had girlfriends.

Paul still has this sociability. He has a network of friends, at

church, at work and even back in New Jersey, where he returns
for occasional reunions. I've envied this about him. He has always
been good at building relationships, doing people favors—coming
through when necessary by pitching in on a friend's backyard
project, fixing a neighbor's oil furnace or volunteering to help
someone at work get his boat in the water. He has put on more
than a few clambakes for retirement parties and wedding recep-
tions. This web of relationships showed in the construction of the
cabin—he had access to tools, equipment and help when we
needed them. Friendship is important to him. I on the other hand
have lived a rich inner life, but it has been a self-absorbed life. Paul
isn't reflective in the same way. He puts his thinking to work on
solving practical problems—how to renovate the church's parish
house kitchen or help a neighbor start his car. He cooked a big
meal nearly every Sunday for his kids and their friends. On holidays and birthdays, he let each of the eight children pick their
favorite foods for him to prepare.

It was in part this sociability—his ease with people and a straight-
forward engagement with the world and its simple pleasures—
that brought him closer to our stepfather, Johnny. I had only one
or two spasms of resentment about his relationship to Johnny.

The most powerful episode happened when I was about twelve.
We were still living in New Brunswick, our urban interruption
between episodes of life in the country, and Johnny was staying
with us even though he and my mother had not yet married. I
was playing catch with Johnny when a boy who lived in the same
apartment complex joined in. His name was Freddy De Leo, and
he was a terrific baseball player. He was maybe thirteen, athletic
and a little cruel in the way he threw the ball at you, and you had

the sense he was destined for the major leagues. Soon Johnny was throwing him more balls than he was throwing me and complimenting Freddy on his arm. Eventually I was getting no balls thrown to me. I held back my tears until I reached the inside of our first-floor apartment. My mother saw me crying and asked me why. I told her. She ordered me to stop. It was unmanly, she said. That was the word she used: "unmanly." Now I felt inadequate in the eyes of both my mother and Johnny, and I blamed Paul—maybe because I knew he would not have cried. Even then I understood he was stronger in that way. For about an hour I wanted to hurt him, and I concocted plans, but then the urge passed with a powerful feeling of guilt.

These episodes were few, and they eventually stopped altogether even though it was clear Paul held a special position with Johnny. Paul was more of a man's boy—tough, with an attitude, barely skirting trouble, sometimes inviting it. On the other hand, I was quiet and often alone, wanting to be reading or wandering in the woods or fishing, and I would do things Johnny could not comprehend, like asking for a typewriter for Christmas. At moments, I think Johnny, a big strong man whom Paul and I both loved, thought I might be gay. I remember the time, after we had moved down to the shore, that a new neighbor of ours, a former schoolteacher from out of town, suggested that I apply for a scholarship to spend my final two years of high school at a fancy prep school in New Hampshire. Johnny was stubbornly firm that I not go, in a way I had not seen in him before. He feared, I think, that I would tip in the wrong direction and be drawn too easily into a boarding school culture of buggery.

But another reason I overcame the resentment was that I knew

Paul was proud of me. I was sure of this because he was constantly arranging fights for me with neighborhood boys, and I knew Paul well enough to realize that he would not want to be associated with a brother who was a loser. A long straight city street, Lee Avenue, connected our scruffy garden apartment complex in New Brunswick with our elementary school, a four-story brick box with big windows and black iron fire escapes inside a tall chain-link fence. I remember fighting my way down that street on my way home on more than one occasion. I was tall and skinny with a high threshold for pain, and a pretty good fighter, especially once the punching stopped and the other boy and I began twisting on the ground. I had long legs that could scissor my opponents into immobility. My best move was the one I used on Paul: I pushed my opponent's face to the ground and brought an arm around his back and lifted it until the pain forced him to say he had had enough. "My brother can kick your ass," Paul would say, and he was only eight years old. He had stronger words, but that phrase usually sufficed. I hated the fighting but enjoyed my brother's unspoken respect.

As boys, we took the bus to summer day camp together, sang in the child's choir together and swam naked together at the Y, but as we moved into the higher grades, then high school, we occupied different worlds. I moved with the good kids; Paul with the bad, or those on the margins.

It was a difficult period for all of us—the root problem was the same, but the manifestations in our lives were different. My mother had met Johnny while separated from our father when we were small boys, and Johnny lived with us on and off for several years before they married. He usually slept on the couch in those nonmarried years, my mother's gesture toward family morality. As far as Paul and I were concerned, he was tightly and irrevocably inside our family—a combination father and big brother. He always drank a lot, but he was a happy and exuberant man, with a big presence and sense of humor and mischief, and full of surprises and stories. He liked to sing country songs: Hank Williams, Johnny Cash. We were proud of his size and strength, and we craved his attention. He gave it generously, taking us fishing, watching television with us and planning preposterous trips—boat shopping, as if we would ever buy one—in his broken-down cars. Often we ended up in a darkened bar in the middle of the day, and he had us sit next to him, served birch beers by the bartender. Sometimes we played shuffleboard with him in the cool dimness of the tavern. We all loved him, and if it is possible to say who loved him most, that was probably my mother.

Just as I was entering the eighth grade, Johnny and my mother married and bought a house ("Waterfront Living, No Money Down"). He had finally, after long effort, obtained a union card for the merchant marine, but after two years and four extended trips at sea, his drinking had worsened. The money he made disappeared mostly to liquor and there were long periods of unemployment. My mother worked furiously to hold on to the house—I remember the mortgage payment to this day, $166. It was the amount she—we—had to come up with each month for the bank. It was clear by now that Johnny was an alcoholic, unreliable and often sick. He had hard vomiting episodes in the bathroom. Unable to make the payments, we lost the house. By then, I was a junior in high school. We moved to another garden apartment.

I went off to college at seventeen; Paul was then thirteen, entering his first year of high school. When I left, in September 1968, Paul was small, with light brown hair and little hands. When I returned three months later for Thanksgiving, he was bigger, his hair was darker and he was showing signs of a mustache. At college I had been worried about what was happening at home, but Paul was there and experiencing Johnny's descent firsthand. Then one day Johnny was gone. That's it—he disappeared. He had been at home to sleep off a bender. It was New Year's Eve, and my mother had argued with him before she went off to work, a busy day for her as other women prepared for holiday parties. By early evening, when she got home, he had left. No note, no explanation. Just gone.

My mother had by then been near an emotional collapse from worry about money and the conflict with Johnny, and his departure brought her a combination of sadness and relief, setting in motion a long melancholic emptiness that went on for years. It broke her. She experienced his departure as a kind of death after a long illness. But Paul's reaction was angry and violent; he was devastated. He was a junior in high school by then, and he and Johnny had continued to be close, despite the boozing. It was right around this time that Paul got his first motorcycle. It was a 90-cubic-centimeter dirt bike, which is a lot of power for a boy tearing through the woods on sandy paths and between trees. Johnny loved motorcycles—he had owned an Indian as a young man—and he put his big frame on Paul's tiny dirt bike to try it out. Motorcycles were one more way that they related to each other. Johnny's departure—no good-bye, nothing—clobbered Paul. I remember coming home from college and discovering him intent on finding Johnny. He said he would track him down in whatever beer joint he had disappeared into and (he said) beat the shit out of him. It was love turned overnight to rage. How could Johnny have done this to him?

Paul's life pivoted in another way too. As a child, he had been mischievous and unruly. As a teenager, he became politicized, which made his rebellion dangerous. In his sophomore year of high school, a friend handed him a flyer in the school hallway that had been produced by the Students for a Democratic Society. The flyer attacked the Vietnam War. There was a meeting, and Paul attended it with his friend. He found it interesting. In 1969, a half million American troops were in Vietnam, and nearly a thousand were being killed a month. A quarter of a million people marched on Washington to protest the war.

Paul was taking an economics class at the time. He asked the teacher challenging questions about capitalism. This was not part of the day's lesson, the teacher said. Paul persisted. The teacher fumed. "This is an economics class, right?" Paul said out loud. He was sent to the principal's office.

He let his hair grow long. In the summer, he went to rock concerts, mainly in Philadelphia, to see the Rolling Stones, Ten Years After, Procol Harum, Alice Cooper, James Taylor and Bob Dylan. He smoked marijuana and, to the complete consternation of the local police, began dating the daughter of the town's deputy police chief.

I was aware only vaguely of the life he was living. I came home in the summer from college and worked long hot days at a construction job that typically left me so exhausted that I showered and went right to sleep when I got home. Sometimes I didn't even have the energy to shower and I fell asleep in my work clothes.

Then, in the fall of Paul's senior year of high school, there came an event that landed him in serious trouble. A bomb threat was called into the high school while he was in class. Students were evacuated to the gym while the police searched the school. The hundreds of students in the gym were restless and noisy, as they are when they are in a big group and loosely supervised, and the teachers there, too, were talking among themselves and kibitzing. An assistant principal went to a microphone and scolded the students for being noisy. He demanded silence. Paul stood up in the crowded room and said something like, "Why don't you say something to the teachers? They're talking too." The students cheered. A back-and-forth ensued between Paul and the assistant principal. Paul walked out. Incredibly, several hundred students followed. The next day, he was expelled from high school.

My mother called me at college. "They're throwing Paul out of high school. Can you come home?" I came back from New Hampshire, a sophisticated college senior (or so I thought) and English literature major, and made an appointment with the school principal. I brought my mother along. My goal was Paul's reinstatement with a pledge that he would cause no further trouble. This brought weak smiles from the administrators in the room. They countered with a proposition: Paul could finish school but not at Toms River. They offered a GED program in North Dakota where he would also work with Indians to satisfy his desire to work with the oppressed. (Yes, they wanted him on a reservation!) The adventure completely appealed to Paul, and a compromise was worked out. The program would begin in the summer, several months away. They also wanted him away, out of town, in the interim. So he came back with me to college and slept in my room. He found college life amenable and especially enjoyed the parties.

After a month, the high school decided against the Indian program—because of the expense, I think—and he was readmitted to finish his senior year. By then, with encouragement from the school administration, he had come under the surveillance of the township police. He had gotten under their skins too. They waited patiently for him to make the wrong move. Weeks before he was going to graduate, he was approached by an older guy at Seaside Heights—the nearby boardwalk resort town where Paul and his friends often hung out. The guy was a Vietnam vet and a local hippie who had a reputation, literally, for having gone to pot. He wanted to buy some grass. Could Paul help him out? Paul said yes and made a contact for him, and the grass was delivered by an intermediary. A couple of months later, in a sweep through Ocean County, dozens of arrests were made and a warrant was issued for Paul's arrest. The hippie had been a narcotics agent. This was a new order of seriousness. Paul turned himself in to the police.

The cops, of course, were gleeful. He was booked at the Dover Township police station and taken through the various stations of the cross—mug shot, fingerprinting, holding cell. While there and waiting, he saw the mother of one of his friends who worked in the courthouse. Paul said hello. She wanted to know what he was doing at the police station. He told her.

"Oh my," she said.

Paul and her son were close friends. She was one of those no-nonsense and capable women who as secretaries run courthouses, school district offices and probably the offices of congressmen. (I had known many from my mother's beauty shop, where they had their hair done religiously every Thursday. Shampoo and set.) She said she would see what could be done. Two days passed. She got back to him: the police would be willing to file the charges with no prosecution but without dismissal if he left Toms River for at least a year and enrolled in college. This was a deal even a DA would have had trouble arranging.

So off he went to Monmouth College, majoring in sociology and discovering Marcuse, Marx and the Grateful Dead. He lived with a group of guys in a big house in Long Branch, just around the corner from the Stone Pony bar in Asbury Park, where a singer and guitar player named Springsteen was getting started. It was there that he met the dark-eyed beauty from Philadelphia, and the two of them organized demonstrations against the war at Fort Monmouth down the road from the college. My mother sent me the clippings from the *Asbury Park Press*. One of her sons was in the newspaper, which was not nothing.

CHAPTER 6

THE FRAME

I had been stubborn about salvaging the timbers because I knew that no part of this cabin would give me more pleasure than assembling its frame. In an odd way, the urge to raise those timbers was rooted in my need to put my life back together, or at least the pieces of it that had felt broken. I don't know how I had connected these two impulses, to build and to reorder my life, or how a spark was made to arc between them, but there was no mistaking the satisfying inner hum I felt the moment I brought the work of the cabin, and especially the assembly of the frame, into my thoughts.

It surely was not because I was a born carpenter. Not even close. Neither did I grow up with barns or timber frames. I was a boy who had grown up in coastal South Jersey where there were farm stands and chicken coops, but not barns, and certainly not the stands of big-circumference trees in which were packed the beams to build them. My boyhood timber was scrub pine, swamp cedar and spindly sassafras. I can't even recall precisely, down to the actual barn, the first time I saw a timber-frame structure. It must have been in a book or magazine, which is not surprising when I think of the extent to which I had taken from books the ideas about how I might live my life. Books had been my surrogate parents.

My first recollection of an encounter with an authentic timber frame coincided with several crucial vectors in my life: the attempt to make a start as a husband and father, a yearning for a life in the country and a deepening appreciation of an aesthetic whose principal virtue was simplicity. I suspect, too, that my response was wrapped up in some spiritual way with my life then as a reader and the discovery of Tolstoy and his projected self, Konstantin Dmitrievich Levin. I was about twenty when I first read Tolstoy, and each time I finished reading one his stories, I felt as if I needed to recover from the stun of an electric shock. Never had literature spoken so directly to me or had life so fully opened up on the page. The beauty and intimacy of the land, the mix of the vast landscape and the Christianity of the gospels, the mysticism of Mother Russia and the wonder of it all—the sunshine, the rain, the snow, the grass bending before the breeze and of course the Great Man's ability to put all of this into language (at least as it was conveyed to me in those Victorian translations by Constance Garnett)—was a crucial part of me trying to form myself as a young man. I was looking for a code, and his books provided it. For about two years, as I read my way through his novels and stories, I was drunk on Tolstoy.

There was Levin pulling on his big boots to survey the countryside around his farm, or Levin, back bent, in the hot sun with scythe in hand:

Another row, and yet another row, followed—long rows and short rows, with good grass and with poor grass. Levin lost all sense of time, and could not have told whether it was late or early now. A change began to come over his work, which gave him immense satisfaction. In the midst of his toil there were moments during which he forgot what he was doing, and it came all easy to him.

I was impressionable, and as I say, I had built an awful lot of my life out of books. My other hero out of Tolstoy at the time was Father Sergius, the dashing military officer who forswore a brilliant career at court to become a monk, and who after retreating into asceticism fell again to pride and temptation. I sometimes wonder if a different reading list would have made me a different person. In any event, the Russian with the big boots, tunic and long beard had prepared the ground for a lot of my decisions that followed. What was happening on that hillside was the continuation of something that had begun when I was a young man looking for a way to lead my life.

All of which is to say that for me a timber frame is nothing so much as an aspiration toward an idea—in the same way that a Japanese teahouse is an idea or the Parthenon is an idea or even a well-constructed bait shack at the end of a pier is an idea. It is a conception with both aesthetic and practical implications for the people who use it or live in it. In the case of my cabin, the idea was humble, but it had the benefit of being built on a hillside in Maine with wood sawn from Maine trees. Surely there was some virtue in its origins. Didn't Tolstoy put simplicity in the same company as goodness and truth?

My nephews and I had stacked the timbers near the cabin before the snow had fallen. So while the stack had to be shoveled off each weekend, at least it was handy to the job. The timbers weighed between fifty and two hundred fifty pounds each, depending on the dimensions, the density of the wood and the amount of water they had absorbed. The posts and beams were six inches square and up to sixteen feet long; the rafters were six inches by ten inches and fourteen feet long.

The first task for Kevin and me was to take stock of our materials. The timbers had been cut in different ways to serve a variety of structural purposes, and the differences were in the dimensions and the idiosyncrasies of the joinery. We had corner posts with shouldered mortises on adjacent surfaces and running posts with mortises on opposite surfaces. We had beams with tenons that would fit these mortises, and beams that did not. Then we had rafters with tongues and others with forks so that they would fit together right and left at the roof's peak.

Post-and-beam carpentry owns a vocabulary every bit as rich and arcane as that of nineteenth-century seamanship. There are scarf joints, dovetail joints, housed dovetail joints, laps and half laps, knee-brace joints and bird's mouths. Each serves a distinct purpose. In Japan, where timber-frame carpentry is a thousand-year-old craft, master framers have developed four hundred different ways of joining timbers for strength and beauty. One simulates the neck of a goose. The Japanese have a term, *kodama*, "the spirit of the tree," to describe this art; their timber framers make roofs that look like hands in prayer or an emperor's hat floating in the air. In New England, which drew on its European roots for building methods and adapted old-world practices to the abundance of virgin forests, housewrights adhered to a half dozen joints, building sturdy capes, saltboxes, barns and churches from native pine and oak. And just as every sail on a Yankee clipper ship had a name for the practical purpose of efficient seamanship, so it is with every timber in a timber frame: there are girts, girders, struts, beams, summer beams, purlins, collar purlins, crown posts, king posts, queen posts, collar ties and ridgepoles.

All this complexity and craft immediately appealed to Kevin. He was never happier than when he was sorting something: tools, materials, techniques. Now he was also learning a new vocabularly to match the work. We pulled timbers from the pile and arranged them on the deck. The deck also had to be shoveled off and swept, and while the snow was piling higher, it still had not yet topped thirty-two inches, the distance between the ground and our raised work surface. But it was getting close.

Nearly all the joinery work for the cabin had been done for us by that long-ago carpenter. Our challenge was to lay his conception of the cabin over my more recent intentions. This would require some new joinery to accommodate the discrepancies of vision, but mostly our work was to sort the pieces, connect them into bents and raise them into place to make our box. It was plenty of work for two men, both brain work and back work, especially since one of the men was not as strong and limber as he used to be. We fitted the tenons into the mortises, tightened the pieces together with a ratchet and pulley and pegged the joints with oak dowels when we had the angles at square. We raised the first bent at the far end of the cabin, and after taking a suitable amount of time to admire our achievement, realized the need for the first major adjustment. The long-ago carpenter had designed beams that ran from bent to bent at midwall height. Those horizontal beams would make it impossible to put in my tall windows. I wanted tall windows, nearly floor-to-ceiling windows, for lots of light. I had stayed in a nearly windowless trapper's cabin once, and it was like living in an old shoe. I had no desire to be a shoe dweller. I wanted cascades of sunshine falling on my buttery pine floors and lots of fresh air and balsam scent pouring in through the windows.

"We don't need them," Kevin declared, having already grasped the way in which this framing worked. "We've got plenty of rigidity with the top plate and the siding. I say we ditch them."

I agreed.

Neither had the carpenter's original conception anticipated an ell to the structure. As we had discovered when we audited our materials and examined the joinery, he had designed one big cabin and two smaller cabins. He had been true to my "family compound" exhortation. We modified his big cabin, making it longer, and reconceived one of the smaller boxes as the ell. We decided to fit them together at the front of the cabin, to the right (facing the front). We measured and cut the beams for the ell, then chiseled and shaved our own mortises and tenons to connect the ell, at a right angle, to the main part of the cabin. This reconception, excluding one of the smaller boxes, would mean lots of leftover beams, and already the prospect of a small barn was planted in my mind.

Kevin and I did this work in the weeks before and after Christmas. We drove up from Portland, and sometimes we stayed at the inn. It was an enjoyable time for me. I liked his company and conversation, and I was getting to know him better. We imagined summer weekends at the cabin, filling it with family, and cooking outdoors, fishing in the nearby streams and swimming in the lake. The talk appealed to both of us, especially after an exhausting day when our muscles were sore and the conversation kept us engaged in the cabin without having to lift one more heavy beam. The conversations ranged wider, though mostly I was listening and giving Kevin the space to open up. I had been away from him nearly seven years, when I was in Philadelphia, and he had done a lot of growing up in that time. He described the trouble he had been in and the heartache he had caused his father. "My dad has done a lot for us kids," he said. "I think it's time for us to show our appreciation better." As he itemized his scrapes with school and the law, I realized that I had been an absent uncle as he had moved through a difficult period of his life. I felt another stab of regret. It had been selfish of me to be so involved in my own problems that I had not gotten involved in my nephew's. But it also occurred to me that the cabin, even before it was built, was helping me to know him better and giving me a chance, even at this late date, to offer some counsel and support.

These conversations, easy and natural, were as good for me as they were for him. It was clear that he was proud of his father, and disappointed in a lot of what he had done to upset him. When he got down on himself, I told him some of the hell-raising stories of his father growing up. He listened intently. He seemed not to know much about Paul's past. I left nothing out because it was a history showing that, while Paul had been wild when he was young, the main elements of his character, then and now, were generosity, reliability and steadiness. "Your dad got in every bit as much trouble as you," I told him. "And look at him now." Kevin seemed to take heart from his father's experience. He was quiet for a while. Then he told me he was worried about his father and that he seemed to be under a lot of stress. "Paulie and me haven't helped, I know, getting in trouble and all," he said. "But he seems to have a lot on his mind right now." I told him I worried that I had put even more pressure on him by asking him to help with the cabin.

"No way," said Kevin. "It's something he likes." Kevin suggested there was more conflict at home, in Paul's marriage, than I had been aware of. "Thank God he has the cabin," Kevin added. "It's a good escape for him."

I was glad to hear this from Kevin, because I had begun to think just the opposite—that the cabin was taking too much of his time and had set down one more burden on him, which might have accounted for his absence. Now I could see that those absences were due to the time he needed to deal with issues at home. It wasn't all work or the church.

One morning, soon after Christmas, Kevin and I arrived at the hillside to find twelve inches of new snow. It was light and fluffy, as if the heavens had dropped a load of dandelion puff on the deck and the beams. We didn't need shovels, and it offered no resistance to our brooms; we could have almost blown it off the deck. We had sunshine and cold dry air when we worked in those days before the new year. It was an invigorating atmosphere: hard work, clean downy snow and icy air. Kevin lifted, climbed, sawed, drilled and always cleaned up when we were done—another characteristic of his father. He kept going when I had to rest. My body reminded me often that I was not twenty-four years old, as I had been when I had built the house. I felt stiff in my shoulders and the small of my back was sore. It wasn't so easy to bend under a board or hoist myself onto the deck. I got in the habit of taking ibuprofen every morning before we got to the cabin.

We finished the basic frame, without the rafters, by the end of January. It was another proud moment in the cabin's construction, but we were going to need help to get the rafters in place, and to truly have a completed frame. The rafters were big and heavy, and the work was overhead. It would be clumsy and even dangerous for two men. Fortunately, Paul was ready to rejoin the project.

If I were to make a list of lessons learned about cabin building, one of them would be: order your materials well in advance of when you need them and have them delivered in proximity to the building site.

The late construction of the driveway and the problems of the foundation holes had thrown me off, and I did not follow the advice I would have given to others. The floor-frame lumber had been delivered to the top of the drive before the heavy snow, but now we needed lumber to fill in between the big timbers of the walls and roof. It would have to be dropped at the bottom of the driveway, which was a good two hundred yards from the cabin, and the snow was falling regularly now, piling ever higher. It was well over the deck, by at least a foot.

With Paul back on the job, we began planning for a big day of work. We e-mailed between Boston and Portland. Paul was pushing me to make sure all the materials were at hand and to make my final decisions on the placement of the doors and windows and how I wanted to handle the framing of the roof. He did not want to begin the discussion at the job site. He wanted it settled so the work would fly when we were there.

"Do we have a game plan for Saturday?" he wrote to me. "I want to make sure we have everything lined up so we can make good use of the time."

I assured him of the plan and explained the details right down to the number of pieces of lumber I had ordered for delivery before we would arrive. I called the lumberyard in nearby Oxford and ordered eighty-six two-by-fours and thirty sheets of plywood. The two-bys would frame the walls, and the sheathing would cover them. Paul suggested in a return e-mail that we frame the walls first for strength before installing the rafters overhead. He reminded me to add nails to the lumber order, which I did—two fifty-pound boxes, one of sixteen-penny common nails and another of eight-penny. "I'd have them also bring a bundle of shim shingles," he wrote. "Those will allow us to frame all the exterior walls a standard height and shim to the horizontal bent just in case things aren't level or square." He told me that he was going to load the truck after he got home from work with tools, a generator, the staging and the window frames that were still in the backyard. He already had attached the trailer to bring a snowmobile up, and he was planning to build a sled in his garage that we could pull behind the snowmobile to get everything, including the lumber that had to be delivered at the bottom of the snow-filled drive, to the cabin site.

I had worked on a summer ditch-digging crew when I was in high school, and the foreman would say to us, "Okay, boys, I don't want to see nothing but assholes and elbows."

That foreman would have been blinded and pleased by the blur of men and materials had he been at the hillside on that Saturday in February. Paul arrived with two snowmobiles and a sled, which consisted of a piece of scrap plywood screwed to two old water skis. He also had Kevin and his friend Russell with him, and Russell's bird dog Abby. So there were four of us, and Abby, all charged up for the work. Abby was charged up mostly for running up and down the hill behind the snowmobiles. We hustled the lumber up the hillside. It took all morning and a half dozen trips, with the heavy-duty snowmobile groaning against the loads and the homemade sled fishtailing behind it as we tried to keep the lumber from falling off. A couple of times it did fall off.

A good three feet of snow covered the ground. The day was sunny and cold, with a stiff wind out of the northwest. I had noticed on many of my trips to the hillside that the wind seemed to blow harder and more often here than in coastal Portland and even other parts of Stoneham and nearby Lovell. I surmised some sort of tunneling effect from the nearby mountains and did not give the reason or implications much more thought, but it was apparent when the maple trees swayed and their frozen branches clicked against the winter sky that this was an unusually windy location. We were bundled against the cold, and even with the rigors of bringing the lumber up and down the hill, we needed hats and gloves. While the absolute temperature was around twenty degrees, the windchill was at zero or below. It kept us moving.

By now, in the chronology of construction, I had settled on the positions of the windows in the cabin's walls, and I knew the heights and widths of the used ones I had scrounged. For the few that remained for me to buy, I worked with standard sizes. The information was necessary to lay out and assemble the stud walls.

Russell was a good carpenter. You could tell by looking at him: quality work boots, carpenter's jeans, layered parka and shell, blue Polartec gloves, a nail apron tied smartly at his waist and a thick pencil pushed up into his wool cap. Polite and soft-spoken, Russell seemed always well groomed, even when he was cabin building. As a young man, he had worked with his father building post-and-beam homes down around Freeport and up the coast. He knew his way around a framing square. Russell had been a commercial real estate property manager when Paul had met him a half dozen years earlier, and now he had his own set of businesses: a two-person mortgage finance company (an office assistant and himself), a small restaurant and a couple of mobile home parks. Paul and Russell had an easy rapport, and I was struck by Paul's ability to kid and quip with irreverence among his friends. I could see that Russell, like many others, enjoyed being around Paul—his confidence, his lack of anxiety, his humor and steadiness. It seemed like we all leaned on him.

"Why don't you lay out walls, and call out what you want for cuts," Paul said to Russell. "I'll run the saw."

Kevin and I were going to be secondary actors on this day, gofers. Paul directed Kevin to do the nailing. My role was to answer Russell's questions about the placement of the windows and doors and bring Paul the two-by-fours as he needed them. I also stepped the cut pieces to Kevin as they fell from Paul's saw so Kevin could nail them without interruption. We built the two-by-four walls on the deck and then lifted them into place, fitting them between the posts and beams.

As a formal matter, I was overseeing the job, but as a practical matter Paul had taken over and was directing the work, an important distinction. He had thought through the flow of tasks. I was happy to concede to him the role of skipper of the vessel. I noticed a subtle but important second shift: through the previous month, it had been Kevin and me working together and running the job. Now Kevin had moved to a lesser role—an assistant to the expert players, Paul and Russell. Kevin chafed at this, I could see, and he resented the directions he was being given. Paul was telling him how to nail the two-by-fours and correcting his errors. "That's not how you pull a nail," Paul said. Paul showed him—he laid the hammer flat and rolled the nail out. Kevin disputed some of the advice, but Paul's experience and authority overruled Kevin's objections. Kevin's temper was beginning to rise. I saw that a quiet father-and-son drama was playing out: Kevin wanted to impress his father with his work, and even more deeply to have the work he was doing demonstrate that he had turned a corner in his life; Paul, for his part, was playing the skeptic, making it clear that one day's work was not sufficient evidence of a new path. At the right moment, I caught Kevin's eye, winked and smiled. I let him know that I was aware of his plight, and that my advice was to let it go. Russell also had picked up on the friction between the two of them and pushed back a bit on Paul by suggesting, with humor, that Paul's cuts could be more accurate.

"Hey, Paul, what are you drinking over there? This stud's a full half inch short," he said.

I had planned to place windows in all of the cabin's walls except for the one wall in the ell that faced the porch. The biggest windows, a full four feet by five feet with the eight-over-eight panes, would go in the front wall of the ell and the back wall of the main living area of the cabin. They would give maximum views to the outdoors. Then I spread tall but narrower windows in all the other walls with the exception of the short right-side wall, where we had left in the one midwall beam, the mistake we had discovered that had us rethink the carpenter's original design. That wall got two smaller windows, on the high side of the beam. I also planned to put windows near the peak on the gable ends of the cabin.

It was astonishing to see the difference that the stud walls with framed-in windows made to the appearance of the rising cabin. It was filling in and looking like shelter. I walked the deck, evaluated the space that would be enclosed by each room and counted the steps from room to room. It was ten steps from the room I'd designated as my writing room to where the door would eventually open from the kitchen to the porch. It was fourteen steps from end to end of the cabin. This was fun. The hammers pounded. At around four p.m., the sun made its descent behind the hemlock trees on the knoll at the rear of the cabin. Kevin and Russell had commitments, so we packed up for the day. I drove back to Portland with Kevin, and Paul and Russell left in Paul's truck, hauling the snowmobiles. Later Paul and I picked up some dinner in Portland and went to bed early.

I woke at six a.m. on Sunday, still full of the good feeling of the previous day's achievement. I slipped out of Paul's house just as it was getting light and drove back to the cabin. There was a thin layer of new snow. I brushed it from the deck and picked up board ends and nails that we had left during the previous day's work. I stood in front of each roughed-out window opening and assessed the view. From the big window closest to where the woodstove would sit, I saw the rising knoll and its hemlocks behind the cabin. This would be the window that would catch the setting sun in winter. From the window of the room where I planned to put my desk, in the right rear of the cabin, I looked out on the big red pines and the slope toward the distant ridge-line. We had not framed in the ell, but I speculated anyway on the views through the big windows that I had planned for its front wall—an oblique line down the hillside through the oaks and maples to the crease where the small brook was now bubbling under the snowpack. The bathroom would have two windows: a view from the toilet to the ledge out back, and from the tub to a collection of small pines, a place where I often saw chipmunks darting in warmer months. They would provide good entertainment during a long soak. I walked to the space on the deck, to the front right, where I would put the kitchen. Its windows would pick up shards of light from the pond below, now just a snow pasture with the tops of reeds showing through the deep blanket of white.

I drove back to Boston, feeling awfully good, and sent Paul an e-mail when I arrived. Me to Paul:

I got up to the cabin early this morning. The work looked great. I covered the lumber with a tarp and picked up the site a bit. Just got home this minute.

Paul to me:

I think the place will really fly from here. I see two, maybe three more productive weekends of work before you can start closing it in. I don't see any reason why it can't be habitable this summer. It's going to be a nice getaway.

Me to Paul:

> I've relied on you a lot for this, and don't let me rely too
> much and take advantage of your good nature. I know
> you've got a lot else on your mind. Probably more than I
> realized. Kevin and I had a nice talk on the way back—I
> enjoy these trips with him. He's really looking forward to
> coming up in the summer and taking the boat out on Kezar
> Lake. I see so many good impulses in him, and brains.

Paul to me:

> Kevin has a lot of potential; this project is a huge confidence
> builder for him and all of this is great for his psyche; Andrew
> just e-mailed me a picture of a boat he wants me to go halfs
> with him on. Will probably do it. It would be a good boat to
> haul up to Kezar Lake for a day of fishing out on the lake.

I spent the next month filling in the two-by-four framing,
mostly alone. My old solitary self was fully engaged on these
weekend trips. It was a lifelong habit, being alone.

Solo work has always appealed to me. My favorite activities
have been solitary pursuits: fishing, walking, reading and writing.
Each of these activities has offered me antiphonal moments of
effort and ease, concentration and relaxation. They also accommodate my tendency to daydream, and occasionally I caught myself taking a long mental walk around some idea that had occurred
to me as I was working. The experience was entirely pleasurable,
if not always productive. Antisocial? Maybe a little. Misanthropic?

Not at all. I brought a better self to my encounters with others after a period of sustained solo work. So to my list of pleasant solo occupations, I now added cabin building. Alone with myself, I took my time with each building task, thinking it through lightly, letting myself feel the materials, visualizing the conclusion.

The other benefit of these periods alone is the erasure of time. While fishing, for example, an intense couple of hours spent approaching, studying and casting a fly to a single feeding trout might compress into the sensation of a few brilliant seconds. It is an experience not so much out of time as before time—before the careful ordering of tasks and responsibilities turned daily consciousness into a chronometer of looming responsibilities. I was discovering these same pleasures of undistracted and pure concentration in the carpentry the cabin required. These moments were temporary escapes, but they were powerfully cleansing and restorative. I was even adding a little muscle.

Usually, I would go up on a Saturday morning, work along easily, and then drive five or six miles to Melby's, a country restaurant at the top of the hill in North Waterford, where I'd sit at the Formica counter and order the world's best fried haddock sandwich. I passed the end of February 2009 this way, and the beginning of March, too, and I witnessed the turning of the season, from deep and implacable winter to a shallower collapsing winter that was struggling to let it be spring. The north country year does not have four seasons. It has more like twelve: winter, spring, summer and fall, each a triptych with a slow start, a glorious peak and an ambiguous conclusion.

If you are attentive to the light, and the taste and feel of the air, it even is more like sixteen seasons. Winter is easily parsed into four seasons: cold and wet, cold and snowy, bitter cold, softening cold. These follow a sine curve not unlike the shallow course of the winter sun. I was in the phase of softening cold: the tips of the once long shadows of the trees were creeping back toward the tall trunks as the pale sun traveled higher in the sky; the snow was deep but it was gray and it was sunken around the bases of the dark hemlocks; and I could hear the hammering of male woodpeckers resounding through the woods around the cabin. They were banging their heads against hard surfaces to impress the females.

The winter of deep snow, now ending, no doubt had been a blessing to the mice and other small mammals that had lived safely under the smooth white blanket and among the winterberry leaves, insulated from the cold and, more important, hidden from the famished owls that watched and listened from above. Of course, in the natural cycle of things, the temporary respite from overhead danger would mean a good year for the foxes and fisher cats come spring. Then it would be their turn to prosper.

The loggers who had cut over the hillside before I bought my piece of land had brought their equipment up an old logging trail that followed the line of the ridge behind the cabin. Theirs may have been the fourth, fifth or sixth cutting since the first settlers' axes felled the stands of virgin timber on these hills. I often walked the trail because of the view it afforded at its highest point to the hardwoods covering other hillsides to the north and Kezar Lake to the east, and because it nearly always showed the tracks of moose and coyotes. The logging crew had done its work selectively and with care, taking out most but not all of the biggest trees and leaving the medium and small trees standing, including oaks and maples that eventually would grow into valuable timber. The woods looked opened up but not ravaged. It was not a clear-cut. It had been responsibly done.

I was curious about what the harvest had yielded and drove to nearby Greenwood, a small town between Stoneham and Norway, to talk with the owner of the logging company that had done the work. His name was Wayne Field, and he had been Rick Rhea's partner in the enterprise of buying, dividing and selling the land. Field, forty-nine, is a tall lean man with smooth muscled arms, wide shoulders, fine straight hair, a goatee and wide glasses. I had no trouble believing he could boss a logging crew. He lived in a log home with a stunning view across a broad valley with a distant meandering stream down its keel. He met me at the door and offered a chair at his kitchen table. I sat down. He gave me a long stare. It would be an understatement to call him intense. He fixed his eyes on me; his face was expressionless; the seconds passed.

"Are you a liberal?" he asked.

There was nothing for me to do but answer honestly that I was a liberal, at least in some respects.

"Teachers are often liberals," he said. Another stare. "Liberals are wrecking this country," he said. "They encourage people to sit on their fat asses, eat potato chips, watch television, get obese and take handouts." He paused. "Hardworking people have to pay for this."

I said I wasn't in favor of handouts.

He had to work hard for everything he had, he said. "Liberals are idealists. It doesn't work."

It was my turn to pause. I thought of the high-quality way he had cut over the hillside. "Liberals," I said, "can be idealists. So can others. In a way, you're an idealist."

"You're giving me smoke and mirrors," he said.

And so it went for about a half hour. He was dead serious and his intensity did not waver. Eventually, I asked him about the hillside. He lightened a little.

"Your land over there wasn't quite ready to be cut," he said. "We did an improvement cut. We removed the lower-grade trees. That's how you grow a nice forest. I don't want to be known as a liquidator, taking everything that you can and putting it on the market to get what you can for it. I believe there is a balance to be had."

Field's company is Central Maine Logging, one of the largest in the state south of Bangor. He employs twenty men and cuts one hundred tons of wood a year. He owns ten cable skidders, five grapple skidders, three chippers, three slashers, one feller buncher and seven pulp trucks. This is about six million dollars worth of heavy equipment. To make payments on the equipment and meet his payroll, he needs to haul about twenty pulp-truck loads of wood a day to mills, logging yards and lumber companies.

"I grew up in a logging family," he said. "My stepfather and brothers were loggers." He said he hoped his sons would take over his business when he retired. "I get out in the morning and look across the frost-covered hills, and I ask myself, 'How lucky am I?' I love what I do."

I asked what he had cut from the hillside where I was building. He said his crew had cut twelve species of trees: red oak, white pine, yellow birch, white birch, spruce, hemlock, beech, red maple, rock maple, ash, black cherry, hornbeam, butternut and aspen. He named them off the top of his head. I was impressed, and I told him that I had always had some difficulty distinguishing between red and white oak. He responded that the difference was in the leaf. The red oak leaf has pointy lobes, the white oak rounded lobes. For him, this obviously was elementary.

Each species of tree they cut had been sorted by grade, he said, and sold for its highest use. The high-grade red oak went for veneer and saw logs, nearly all of it to Canada, but some of it for furniture at the Ethan Allen mill in Vermont. The low-grade wood went for pallets. The good pine went for lumber. Same with the spruce. The lower-grade softwood went to pulp and chips. The pulp was turned into paper; the chips were burned to generate electricity at a biomass plant in Livermore Falls. The beech went for pallets and chips. The ash was shipped to a furniture mill in Canada. The black cherry also was a lumber tree, for furniture, and again it went to Canada. The hornbeam and butternut were chipped. The aspen went to a pulp mill in Jay to be made into glossy paper. (The paper, I later learned, was used in *Cosmopolitan, Seventeen, Redbook, Forbes* and the *New York Times* magazines and for fast-food wraps and microwave popcorn bags.)

I remarked that the high-grade wood seemed mostly to be going to Canada for furniture production. Yes, he said, the buyers of wood in the area had greatly diminished. Nearly all of the mills had closed down. He could remember being able to sell to wood-turning mills in nearby Bethel and West Paris. Those mills had been shuttered. I did some checking and learned that Norway and South Paris, the nearby commercial center for the region, had once hummed with mills making all sorts of wood products; South Paris had once had a national reputation as "Toy Town," with the country's largest concentration of toy makers. Children's sleds were a specialty. These towns—emblematic of others in Maine, the state where the mass-produced wooden toothpick had been invented—had once been thriving manufacturers of wood products. Maine mills made dowels, clothespins, tongue depressors, golf tees, packing crates and thousands of other products from its abundant trees. Nearly all of those small mills have closed down since the 1950s. The loss of that small-scale manufacturing had a devastating impact on the economy of the region—jobs were lost, wages fell, money for local schools diminished and young people moved away.

Field blamed the loss of the mills on Canadian government subsidies and liberal employment laws in the United States. He is partly right, but the picture is more complex. The world changed while Maine mostly stayed the same: low-wage and wood-rich parts of the world took the business; the buying patterns of giant international retailers favored huge producers over small local ones; and new materials, mostly plastic, became a substitute for wood.

But the land has continued to grow trees in abundance, and some men, who inherited the skills and took naturally to the work, have continued to cut them.

Wayne Field's crew of five men had spent three weeks at the hillside in October and November of 2007 felling, limbing and yarding the trees, and they had hauled fifty loads of logs and chips worth about $75,000 at the mill, log yard and biomass plant.

I asked him if he would come out to the cabin one day and walk the hillside with me. I needed to improve my tree-identification skills. He said he would be happy to. I gathered my coat and notebook to leave, and he showed me some photos of himself and his sons and the deer they had shot. They were impressive, big bucks all of them. We talked some more—he was a coyote trapper. I told him of my muskrat-trapping days. I thought I detected a smile. He brought some more photos. Finally, we shook hands and said good-bye and I drove back to Boston.

Paul, Kevin and I regrouped in the middle of March, with one week, by the calendar, left in winter. We completed the framing and moved to the rafters, which was hard and serious work. Kevin was still unemployed, so he remained engaged in the project, to my good fortune but not his. He had been picking up occasional part-time work on a maintenance crew at Portland City Hall. As usual, Paul had given the work a lot of thought. His judgment was that we should first build and then position the lighter rafter assemblies, the two-by-six trusses, which we were adding for strength and reliability to the roof between the massive timber rafters. The plan was to assemble them on the deck, and three of us, with Kevin up in the high staging, would raise them to the top plate of the wall. First one end of the rafter assembly went up to the plate, then the other end, and then with a rope we (Kevin) hauled the peak upward. Once the assembly was in place and plumb, we nailed it to the plate; after the first one went up, we nailed boards across the surface of them for bracing. Our plan was to bring the big rafters up into place once all the lighter rafters had been secured. At the end of the first day we had eight light trusses in place.

On the following Saturday, Paul and I returned to assemble the rest of the trusses. Paul wasn't feeling well. He had the beginnings of a cold, a headache and a sore throat. He decided to come anyway. I had tried to reach Kevin, but he was not answering his phone. I guessed he had had a rough night; Paul said that was most certainly the case. The day brought several snow squalls—the snow came down so rapidly at times and in such big flakes that we could barely see the frame from one end to the other; other times the sun was out and the day sparkled like a palace chandelier. The wind blew with hardly a pause, but we pulled our hoods over our heads and turned our faces away from the weather and continued to work. I stopped only to wipe the snow from my glasses. It was sticky wet snow, like the cottony puffs of wind-borne seeds, and the flakes attached to whatever they touched. It was a joy to be out in it, but I worried about Paul and his cold. He said he was fine and worked right along. We needed to be careful not to slip on the slick surface of wet snow the intermittent squalls were laying down on the deck. At day's end, all of the trusses were assembled and neatly stacked, ready for hoisting atop the walls.

There is a curved line of mountains west and north of the cabin. The closest ones, to the west, are about a half mile distant—Joe McKeen, Stiles, Adams, Rattlesnake and Palmer mountains. They are named for early settlers, except for Rattlesnake. To the west and north, in the bend, are Speckled, Durgin and Butters mountains. Durgin and Butters were men who came into this country early too, and one of the later Durgin boys, a sergeant in the Union Army, helped carry the coffin of Abraham Lincoln. His grave is about two miles from the cabin. These mountains share a rugged fifteen-mile ridgeline, like the spine of some skinny and

curled-up cat. It may be the ladlelike shape of the hills that captures the wind as it comes down from the north and then bends
it, either speeding it up or spinning it into high-speed eddies that
barrel past the cabin on the way toward Kezar Lake. Stoneham
residents have told me about brief powerful windstorms in and
around the west shore of Kezar Lake, sometimes accompanied by
thunder, that have laid a hillside of trees as flat as the spines on a
porcupine's back.

I knew none of this weather history when we made our next
trip to the cabin to resume work on the rafters. I was aware only
that I was building in a windy spot and that we had been sure to
brace the rafters when we had left the previous Saturday. I dis-
tinctly remembered nailing scrap two-by-fours across their tops
for added rigidity. I walked up to the cabin ahead of Paul and
Kevin, shuffling through the snow. From the path, the cabin does
not come into view until the second turn, and then only barely
through the trees. At the second turn, the cabin is back fifty yards
into the trees and a full ten feet above the head of someone walking up the path. It is in the third turn that the cabin presents itself
in full view, and it was there that I looked up to assay the work
we had accomplished.

At first, I was confused by the sight of it, sensing only that
something was wrong, and then I focused on what was wrong and
saw the disaster that had occurred. All of the rafters we had erected
had been knocked down. Some of them lay flat across the tops of
the walls, and others had dropped all the way to the deck. One of
the beams, at the far end of the cabin, had blown out and was
lying in the snow. Apparently the trusses, which were big heavy

triangles, had acted as wedges as they collapsed, forcing apart the timbers.

I was taking this in when Paul came up behind me.

"Catastrophe," I said.

"What?"

"Have a look."

We walked up together.

"Son of a bitch," I said. I walked among the welter of twisted lumber.

Paul looked at me and smiled. "Well, what's a construction job without at least one disaster?" He was oddly upbeat. "We can fix it."

Kevin, who had been lugging the generator up the hill, now joined us on the deck. "What happened?" he asked.

"It must have been one hell of a wind," I said.

The sky was gray and threatening rain, which might come down as sleet or cold drizzle at any moment, and here I was confronted with the loss of all our overhead work and damage to the frame. I had been worrying all week about the harm that rain—rather than snow—might do to the deck if the roof didn't soon go up. If the deck's plywood were to get wet, and stay wet, it would begin to delaminate. It would have to be torn up and replaced with new plywood—more time and money. I had a diminishing supply of both. It had been dicey but acceptable in the coldest part of the winter to leave the deck uncovered. Snow would not damage it, but now we were moving into a season when it was likely to get wet from melting snow or rain. I had wanted to hurry the roof along in the next couple of days—and now this event, which would delay the completion of the roof even further. How much time would the fallen rafters cost me—a week, two weeks, more?

I told Paul I remembered nailing scrap two-by-fours across the tops of them to prevent them from racking in the wind.

"Yeah, we did," Paul said, "but it wasn't enough for whatever blew through here."

Paul and Kevin seemed not at all set back, and Kevin began working out a way to untangle the mess. He offered his ideas to Paul, who listened and offered some of his own, and the two of them were in deep conference, buoyed by the challenge of it. It was as if they were two mathematicians standing in front of a chalkboard examining a long equation for the errant variable. This is what they liked: problem solving. Finally Paul put forward a rescue plan. We would leave the fallen rafters where they were for the time being, and first we would brace the walls against any further splaying. Then we would go to the opposite end of the cabin and bring into place, atop the wall, the other rafter assemblies we had constructed the previous week, the ones we had yet to set up. Once they were well secured and braced, we would return to the damaged end of the cabin, swing the fallen rafters that had not been twisted too badly back up into position and pull down those that had gotten too mangled. We would build new ones where necessary.

To my astonishment, we had the new rafters in place before noon, and by midafternoon we had repositioned the fallen ones. Kevin was the day's hero. He climbed the staging, walked the top plates and hoisted the fallen rafters with a rope from above with a disdain for height that is the possession only of young men.

"Put a rope on your waist," I told him.

"Nah. I'm alright, Uncle Louie."

"No, Kevin. I'm demanding it." I threw him the rope.

I followed his path on the deck below, reasoning I could break his fall with my body if he came down.

With the rafters back up, Paul insisted that we clean up the job site and cover the deck with a tarp to protect it against the weather. Before we left, we put extra bracing on the rafters, front and back, and we replaced the beam that had blown out. It was a good day's work. We celebrated at Melby's with dinner.

Despite my urgency to get the big timbered rafters in place so the roof could go up as quickly as possible, Paul said no. We needed to sheathe the exterior walls first. The sheathing would stiffen the walls, he said. Even more important, to put the roof on first, ahead of sheathing the exterior walls, would be to turn the cabin into a giant umbrella that would catch the wind and lift the frame off the foundation. "I've seen it happen," Paul said. I pictured the cabin rising over the trees on the wind like a dirigible and then crashing down when the wind stopped. No argument from me—we were building a cabin, not a kite. We would apply the wall sheathing first. In the meantime, I would keep the deck covered with a tarp and do my best to keep water off the subfloor, which was already beginning to show some swelling from moisture around the nail heads.

We used the next few weeks to frame the ell and cut and assemble its rafters—yet more work ahead of the roof. I tried to reach Kevin one Saturday, but Paul told me he had gotten into a scrape overnight and had ended up in the emergency room, where a doctor put twenty stitches in his head. So it was Paul and I, and then Paul and

I and Andrew, who were home on leave for a week. I was thrilled with the progress we were making now. The spring that was emerging filled me with enthusiasm for the work and the hillside. All would be well—even if we were racing the season and the thaw.

I chose a Friday in April to spend my first night in the cabin. There was still no roof cover, and the walls remained unsheathed. In other words, it was a frame, open to the weather. I drove up from Boston, arrived an hour before dark and spread my sleeping bag on the deck. I heard a commotion of splashing on the pond below. It sounded like *slap, splash—slap, splash—slap, splash!* I had to have a look. I walked down the path to the pond and saw one Canada goose madly chasing another. Neither was fully lifting from the water—they were sort of running and flapping over the surface, one clearly in pursuit, the other making his retreat. The splashes looked like machine-gun fire hitting the water. I was witnessing two males in combat over an unseen female. In the mating season, a female goose selects the male based on his ability to protect her, and what was probably occurring in front of me was a powerful male demonstrating his prowess to a keenly observing female. Once geese are paired, the mating is an elaborate ballet. It begins with the male and female facing each other, undulating their long necks and making soft goose sounds, which is like dry wood being rubbed against slate. It is a sound that seems to contain both effort and pleasure. When the moment comes for the act of mating, they go off by themselves, at night and on the water, in a kind of private tryst. The male and female extend their necks horizontally to the water, dipping their beaks. The female spreads her wings over the surface of the water and slightly submerges. Upon completion of copulation, the female bathes herself with the male watching, and then the male bathes himself as she observes. The watery ruckus unfolding in front of me was a prelude to the courtship and promised that I would have fluffy goslings in the pond in another month.

I still had time before dark, and it was too early to crawl into the sleeping bag, so I walked along the Adams Road and turned down Cold Brook, following it downstream. I came to a beaver pond that I had been unaware of. It had been created by a mud dam that held back a small tributary to the brook. A couple of swallows swooped over the water, picking insects out of the air, and then I saw a beaver making his way across the pond, only his big head breaking through the surface. He spotted me and gave me the angry slap. He went down and did not come back up. I waited quietly. I walked a little farther to an open spot near the brook and listened. This seemed to be a perfect place to hear woodcock whistling. It was the time of year for their courtship display of high flights and sudden twisting drops, but I heard nothing except the sweet melody of the peepers, which was its own reward. It is among the brightest and most cheerful sounds of the woods. The sun was setting now, so I headed back. I reached the big pond, and the sun's rays lit the trees along the far shore and sent a red glow over the water's still surface. Once again, I witnessed that incredible bowl of light—this time as it was rapidly losing its luminescence, like a gas lamp that has been shut but whose glow takes a few seconds to extinguish.

I returned to the cabin, taking my time along the way to examine the hillside. I arranged my sleeping bag and slipped into it. The deck was hard, but at least it was flat and without rocks as there would have been had I been sleeping on the ground. I was using my son Adam's sleeping bag, a fancy mummy bag from L.L.Bean. It had a little hood that rolled up into a small pillow. The peepers were singing loudly, and occasionally I felt a cool puff of damp spring air come up from below when the wind lifted. The air smelled of the wet thawing ground and the new season. Somewhere off in the distance I heard an owl's windy nine-syllable hoot: *Whoo cooks for you, whoo cooks for you all?*

The stars shone brightly in the sky, and I watched them through the crossbeams of the cabin frame. It was as if I were looking through the rigging of a sailing ship, maybe a coastwise schooner making its way down the Atlantic shore. I folded my hands behind my head and stared upward. Another gentle damp breeze blew across the deck, and I imagined my cabin lifting into the sky like some heavenly gaff-rigged raft, ascending into the night sky toward the stars, tacking toward Polaris and then hauling south and west toward Orion and bright Betelgeuse, and eastward for a closer look at the planet Saturn, and silently, behind a big spinnaker full of moonlight, sailing home again. I fell asleep to the sound of the geese gabbing away in the pond, here on earth.

CHAPTER 7

SUMMER WORK

I had been away from the cabin for nearly a month, back in temporary disguise as a professor. I had left the hillside in late April just as the black limbs of the swamp maples had pushed out their delicate red flowers, and now, on my return in May, those same lithe trees were showing tender five-pointed leaves. The fiddlehead ferns were fully unscrolled in the wet places, and along the brooks the skunk cabbages were as big as Alaska cauliflower. It was no longer possible, as it had been in winter and late spring, to see into the woods. The deep spaces were filled in with greenery.

I was free to put my hands and back into the work of cabin building for three uninterrupted months. The time spread ahead of me like a gift, an indolence of chosen work in the outdoors. This was pleasure of a high order. I had sketched out a sequence of building tasks and they stood in my mind as orderly as a long row of Indiana corn. If the need came over me—as it might at any moment—I was accountable to no one but myself and could grab my fishing rod and explore some nearby brook for wild trout.

I guessed my conscience would hold me fast to the cabin at least until the roof was overhead, but the combination of pleasurable work and freedom to slack off if I wanted it was delicious.

I splurged and took a room with a small kitchen at the nearby inn for six weeks: clean linen, fresh towels and a good bed. I had packed a box of books for the empty nights: novels, field guides to birds, trees and flowers, and a couple of histories of Maine. There was a small refrigerator, which I filled with eggs, bacon, frozen vegetables and bottles of wine and beer. This was high gypsy living, and I thought of those banged-up men, and sometimes families, from my boyhood down the shore who would occupy beachfront hotels and motels in the off-season when the rents plummeted.

There was a small staff at the inn, and I came to enjoy their company. Megan, the clerk and manager, lived down the road from the cabin with her husband and three children. Martha was the second clerk. She was a cute blonde, hardworking and determined, raising two children on her own. Not long after I arrived, she married a young man from Guatemala who had been part of a Spanish-speaking crew that was clearing brush along rural power lines in the area. The workers had stayed at the inn, and a romance developed between Martha and one of the handsome young men. Four months elapsed between their meeting and the wedding, held in the inn's side yard on a lovely summer day. And there was Kenny, the overnight clerk. He was twenty-two years old, with light brown hair and fine sparse whiskers that were not quite a beard. He had a long face and fine nose, and he reminded me of the boys seen in Civil War daguerreotypes who had enlisted on both sides by exaggerating their ages. Kenny always had a book in his hand, and I soon learned that he was an insatiable and organized reader.

The first time I met him he was reading *The Pilgrim's Progress.* A seventeenth-century English allegory of Christian life struck me as an unusual choice. I asked about it and learned he was working his way through a reading list that he had taken from a book titled *1001 Books You Must Read Before You Die.* It was a peculiar litany of recommended reading, smelling of arcane discernment and fusty British tastes. So far, he had read *The Pilgrim's Progress, Don Quixote, The Unfortunate Traveller, Euphues: The Anatomy of Wit, Gargantua and Pantagruel, The Thousand and One Nights, The Golden Ass, Aithiopika, Chaireas and Kallirhoe, Metamorphoses* and *Aesop's Fables.* He had also knocked off *Jane Eyre, Oroonoko, Little Women* and *Justine,* to mention just a few.

I don't think I could have found a single professor at my college who had read as many esoteric classics. I told him what I was reading—a novel of New England by Russell Banks. I thought he would recognize the setting and characters. He made a note and said he would get a copy. Over the summer, I came to learn that he had attended the high school in Bethel, where, he said, the teachers had not taken much of an interest in him or his hunger for reading. He was living in a mobile home in nearby Albany, the town where he had grown up, with an elderly couple who had taken him in. He had left home in high school over a dispute with his father. "We didn't see eye to eye," he told me in typical understatement. His father was a woodcutter, and his mother and father lived apart. He was active in the Albany Congregational Church and helped serve the church's monthly public suppers.

We spent many nights near the inn's front desk talking about books. One night I told him I was also working my way through Leslie Fiedler's *Love and Death in the American Novel*. He was interested in the book's argument, and I explained that Fiedler, the towering literary critic, had traced the history of the novel to *Clarissa* by Samuel Richardson in the mid-eighteenth century. "Is that the same Richardson who wrote *Pamela*?" Ken asked me. I said that it was. "I read it last year," he said. "Good book."

This small group at the inn welcomed me, and when I returned there at night after a day's work at the cabin and felt the need for company, I made my way out to the desk, poured a cup of coffee from the pot that was always there and found a willing partner in conversation.

My plan was to have the cabin habitable by the middle of July—a new deadline—and then I would move from the inn to the hillside and finish the work as a cabin dweller. The cabin frame, including all of the rafters, was fully complete. Paul, Kevin and I had muscled those giant rafters into place in April. The tasks ahead of me were, in order: sheathing the exterior walls and roof, which still was not done; applying the pine-board siding; framing inside rooms; stuffing insulation between the studs and rafters; laying up the boards for the interior walls and ceilings; and putting down a floor, which would be planks of wide pine. This was a lot. Paul was available on weekends; I was on my own during the week. Kevin, whose driver's license had been suspended, would come with Paul when he could.

On that first morning of work, I made a distressing discovery. It was going to be awfully difficult for me to put up the sheathing on my own. The four-foot-by-eight-foot sheets of plywood weighed around fifty pounds each, and they were ungainly to maneuver. Putting up a sheet required lifting it, getting it properly aligned right and left and up and down and then keeping it in place as I drove the nails. I used my knees, shoulders, head and back, in a variety of poses and contortions, to hold the pieces against the frame, but it was obvious that this was a job for a Hindu god with four arms—or more likely, here in Stoneham, two men. I went looking for a second man. I found him at the inn.

Billy Mann handled the inn's maintenance. This included mowing grass, splitting firewood, unclogging sinks and toilets, rebuilding steps, refilling propane gas tanks, changing lightbulbs and hauling garbage to the dump—about anything that came up. He was fifty-four years old, big in the chest and shoulders, with white-yellow hair and glasses that enlarged his milky blue eyes. His face showed some roseola and a puffiness that suggested high blood pressure, and his hands were large and rough. His usual outfit was jeans, a heavy flannel shirt and camo baseball-type cap. He had a laugh the timbre of which would change slightly to underscore the basic sense of whatever it was he had just expressed—worry, displeasure, optimism, certainty. He might say, for example, "I got an awful pile of wood waiting for me to split out there." His trailing laughter made it clear he was not eager to begin. Or he would say, "I might have to sneak away on Saturday for a little fishing," and then light laughter indicated this was a reward he was looking forward to. I met him at the inn's front counter, where I saw him each morning leaning on his elbow and collecting his jobs for the day. I asked him if he had any interest in working with me at the cabin, after work or on his days off.

"Yeah, I can help you," he said. His laughter indicated a degree of ambivalence, which was understandable since I had not yet mentioned money.

I soon learned that Billy knew how to work. At the cabin, I explained what needed to be done, and he immediately began carrying sheets of plywood to the cabin frame—by himself. I insisted that we do it together, and soon we were putting up the sheathing in rapid order. One of us would hold the sheet and the other would nail it. I noticed that he often became winded and occasionally pulled an inhaler from his pocket. "It's the asthma," he said. He worked thirty hours a week at the inn (at thirteen dollars an hour), so he had some weekdays open to help me, and sometimes he came after work too.

Billy had been born in Lewiston, Maine, an old mill town. His parents had moved to the tiny village of North Fryeburg when he was six months old. He grew up in North Fryeburg with four brothers and three sisters, and he had lived there ever since. It was about ten miles from the cabin. There was one brief foray to nearby Bridgton when he was eighteen and newly married. The marriage lasted one year and produced a son, Bill, who lived in New Hampshire. When the marriage ended, Billy moved back to North Fryeburg. He had grown up fishing and hunting, and on a Saturday in the late spring he could be found somewhere in the hill country, maybe up near Evans Notch, fishing for brook trout. He was a worm dunker. He left high school in his third year to earn money, and through the years he had worked as a truck driver, farmhand, logger, builder, maintenance man and heavy equipment operator. He always tried to have a job, he told me.

Before the inn, his most recent job had been the best paying but most stressful. He had driven a bucket loader at a biomass energy plant in New Hampshire. He made fifteen dollars an hour straight time, and time and a half after forty hours. He received health benefits there. (He did not at the inn.) His job was to scoop the wood chips brought by trucks to the plant and dump them in the hopper, in the proper mix and at the proper rate. A bad mix, one that was too wet, for example, would slow the generation of electricity. It was stressful work, he told me as we put up the plywood. The job required him to work overtime, sometimes thirty additional hours a week. "They were screamers, too," he said. "You couldn't do nothing right." The money was good but the pressure and the hours, he said, had begun to wreck his health. He was smoking heavily. He developed an ulcer, which burst, and he spent a week in Bridgton Hospital, where he nearly died. He went back to the power plant after his recovery, but the ulcer returned so he quit. By then, he had bought a four-wheel drive pickup truck, and the payments were five hundred dollars a month, which he had been able to afford when he was working at the generating plant. His second wife worked at a plant in New Hampshire that manufactured dog collars, but with his reduced hours and pay at the inn, he was struggling to make ends meet, with the truck an especially big burden. It was one of the reasons he had jumped at the prospect of working with me—he needed the money. He was also worried about the heating bill for his home. Heating oil was going for $2.50 a gallon that season. Sometimes the anxiety that the bills brought on was too much, he told me, and the doctor had written him a prescription to help control it. He was also taking pills to control his blood pressure.

We also talked of more pleasant topics. His favorite times were hunting deer with his son Bill, now a mechanic, and deep-sea fishing for cod and haddock down the coast. He lived in a house he had built himself twenty years earlier. He had four children: Bill, from his first marriage; a girl from a relationship following his first marriage; and two girls from his current marriage, one of whom his wife had brought into the marriage but who counted Billy as her father. His house, which I once visited when I drove him home, was on a sandy road not far from the potato fields that occupy the Saco River bottomland where he had worked as a farmhand. It is just about a mile from the location of the house where he grew up.

"There aren't many people who can do what you're doing," he said.

"What do you mean?" I asked.

"I mean there aren't many people who could just build this place the way you are—buying what you need as you go along and, you know, just deciding to build a place, and then going to the lumberyard or hardware store and getting what you need and having the money for it."

I told him that he was right about that, and I felt fortunate I could do it.

I sometimes walked to the cabin from the inn, and the trek would take me through the intervale, which was alive with robins picking up worms from the damp alluvial soil, and along the southwest edge of the pond. In any season, a pond is endlessly absorbing. In late May, the painted turtles pushed their plow-point beaks out of the water, and tiny green leaves—the floating roofs of the pond-weeds that were anchored in the mud below—dappled the surface. On several mornings I spotted a young bull moose, belly deep in the water with a muzzle full of weeds, looking preposterous, slightly puzzled and self-satisfied in the way that only a moose can. These trips, just over a half mile, sometimes took an hour or two. I dallied along the way and rewarded myself with the leisure of observation even before I could claim a single driven nail.

I began some mornings at Melby's, where I was slowly drawn into the town's conversation. There was a general wariness about me at first, especially since I bought the *New York Times*, but it seemed to dissipate as I developed a breakfast routine. I sat at the same stool, always ordered two eggs over easy with dark toast and no butter, and quietly read the newspaper. The talk around me was mostly about the weather, the Red Sox, the latest outrage by the state legislature, logging, farming or the condition of the town roads. These were well-worn subjects. Customers inquired after each other's health, and the responses acknowledged the greeting but revealed nothing: *Can't complain. I'm okay, I guess. Not bad, you? Been worse.*

One morning, a big man, well into his sixties, leaned toward me about three seats down the counter and said, "What do you think of them Sox, huh!" It was an exclamation but it wanted an answer. Clearly a door was being thrown open. I was prepared to handle the weather or the roads, maybe even to weigh in on the state budget, which I might have mischievously suggested was too low given the condition of the state's schools, which in turn would have caused any number of the frugal countrymen around me to choke and blast their eggs across the counter, but at the moment I had no opinion whatsoever about the Red Sox. I had not yet keyed into their play for the season. I was mute for a slow count of five, then responded, "Well, they're something else, aren't they?"

It was a volley of rhetorical ambiguity with no meaning on either side, but it was response enough to show good faith, and he was off and running on the beauty of Josh Beckett's slider, which he had stayed up late into the previous night admiring. I added nothing to the conversation but encouraging assent and wonder at the young man's extraordinary ability with the ball.

I learned over the following mornings that my acquaintance at the counter had been a long-haul trucker, a senior owner operator, and that the trucking company had canceled his contract. "Can you imagine that?" he said. "After all those years, they just cut me loose." He still couldn't grasp the abrupt and coldhearted action. Things like that just did not happen in the United States of America—although, he added with a scornful laugh, he guessed they did now. "After all those years," he said again, still in disbelief. The company had wanted him to work for less pay, he said. He had calculated that he could not afford his rig's payments at the new rate, so he sold the truck and retired. "I tell you," he said as he put a big fat hand flat on the counter, "I miss it." He lifted his frame off the stool and hauled himself out the door.

It was one of many conversations and glimpses I would have of the hard luck and hard work that were facts of life in this remote corner of New England. It set me thinking a good deal over the summer about the country in general. I could not help but connect the headlines in the newspaper to the lives and attitudes of people like Billy, the truck driver and others I would meet who were struggling outside the tightening circle of jobs that provided decent pay and a little security. The cabin was not only teaching me about the hillside; it was giving me an insight into America.

It rained off and on that last week of May. Billy and I worked when we could, he being more insistent than I that we keep going even when the drizzle turned to light and steady rain. There was a big pile of rocks a few yards off from the cabin, overgrown with moss and small trees, and Billy was convinced it was an Indian burial mound. "Used to be a lot of Indians around here, long time ago," he said. "That's how they made their graves." He said he knew of some places where there were Indian markings on the ledges of cliffs, and that he would take me there if I wanted. "I used to find arrowheads and Indian tools all the time when I was picking potatoes," he said. "'Course, the owner made us give them to him. He's got quite a collection. I'm sure he'll show them to you if you want."

In this way, I began to learn the geography and lore of the area, through the prism of Billy's experience. He told me of places to hunt deer and catch rainbow trout where the wardens were unlikely to find you fishing with worms, and about the roads and trails that cut through the mountains. He had lived his entire life in this landscape, in a square maybe twenty miles by twenty miles, and he knew all the trout ponds, smelt brooks, deer trails and hornpout holes.

On the weekends, and some weekdays when he could get away, Paul arrived in his pickup truck and the work flew. More often than not, he had Kevin with him. Kevin was his usual agile, brave and hardworking self. When it came time for us to bring the sheathing to the roof, Paul set an aluminum ladder against the cabin near the stack of plywood. Kevin went to the rafters and, pulling a rope that had been threaded through a hole that Paul had drilled in each sheet of plywood, brought them aloft, along the rails of the ladder, and set them in place. It went as smooth as peeled ash. Paul had procured a nail gun from one of his vendors. It was an awesome machine, which used an electric spark to fire a blast of butane gas that drove a piston, sending the six-penny nails deep into the wood. *Bam, bam, bam.* Nailing had never been so easy.

The cabin was now closing in, with covered exterior walls and a roof. There was an inside and an outside in a way that there had not been before. The timber frame, bare to weather, described the structure's perimeter but had insinuated no distinctions about interior and exterior. Now we had an inside that was definitely distinct from the outside. I did another one of my admiring walk-arounds. The rough cuts on the windows now really seemed like windows, illuminated rectangles in the darker walls, and I felt the interior embrace of the cabin: the walls meeting at the corners and the vaulted ceiling created by the sheathing on the roof. The cabin was quickly becoming a shelter.

It was about this time that a debate ensued among my building team about the layout of the inside. Framed Oxford-style, the proposition would have read something like this: "Resolved, a wall should be constructed creating a separate room at the right rear of the cabin that will be Lou's writing room." Almost from the beginning, I had decided on making a "writing room," a private space inside the cabin to which I could retreat to put words down on paper (or a computer screen if the computer's battery was sufficiently charged). I had decided on a desk, which would be a hardwood door set on sawhorses, and a spartan chair that I particularly liked for the support it gave my back as well as for the hard frame that would help keep me from drifting off to sleep. I had envisioned a built-in bookcase and a single rough bunk for napping when the words weren't cooperating. I pictured a neat bed, with white sheets folded military-style under the thin mattress and a gray wool Hudson's Bay blanket with a couple of yellow stripes. In my imagination, I had even begun to select the books for the bookcase. I would set a good dictionary on a stand, and I had an excellent collection of New England sporting books that would add a nice touch. Next to the bed, on a small Shaker table, would be a volume of Proust. It is my favorite nighttime reading, an experience never fully mastered. The density of his prose inevitably yields for me new subtleties of emotion and thought with each fresh entrance to the pages. I can read and reread it the way I can listen over and over again to Mozart's music for clarinet. It is a plunge into sensation, heartache and rapture. As we sat on nail kegs and sawhorses in the cabin, I did not bring Proust into the debate over the wall, but I did argue that there were bound to be times when all of us would be up at the cabin, maybe playing poker deep into the night, and it would be a good thing to be able to retreat from the din to a room with a door that closed to allow some sleep.

Paulie, home for a couple of weeks from motorcycle school, took the negative position. "Uncle Louie, every cabin we've ever been in has always been wide open. Cabins are supposed to be open. Remember Carroll Gerow's cabins in Aroostook? Always open. You want space. This ain't a house. It's a cabin. It's going to feel closed up and cramped if you put up a wall." He was passionate. "Trust me on this one," he said. He augmented his position with this: "You can put a desk in the bedroom. It's plenty big enough if you want to write."

Paul and Kevin were with Paulie, but they counseled no decision. "Don't put the wall up now," Paul said. "See how you like it. It's a hell of a lot easier to put one in later if you think you want it than to put one in now and then have to take it out."

I could see which way this tree was falling. I delayed making up my mind and after a couple of weeks came around to the no-wall position. Paulie was right, and I realized that a writing room was really just one more bit of writerly superstition, not unlike insisting on exactly the right color paper before starting to work. The open space admitted more conviviality and elbow room. But I held my ground on the need for a closed-in first-floor storage closet, which I saw as necessary for outdoor gear. I wanted a locker where we could put rods, boots, snowshoes, fishing vests, ropes, wool coats and such out of sight and behind a locked door for the periods when I would be absent. The building team was fine with that.

Paul was coming out regularly now to the cabin. I had him back and he was giving me a lot of time. In fact, he was giving me the summer. I looked forward to the appearance of his pickup truck at the top of the driveway. As he stepped from the truck I would meet him and update him on the progress I had made, either with Billy or by myself, and he would inspect the work and make suggestions on what to do next. He was more relaxed than he had been in the spring, when I sensed that he had been preoccupied, and he seemed to be enjoying himself again in the work. But it was clear to me that there was something turning in his life, and I was fairly certain it wasn't good. I knew from Kevin's comments that all was not well at home. I did not push him to talk about it. I remembered, too, Kevin's comments about the cabin being an escape for Paul, and a source of enjoyment. I did not want to disturb his retreat, if that's what the cabin work had become for him.

Paul and I had not had the kind of relationship where we brought our problems or struggles immediately to the surface of our conversations, he even less than I—much less than I. But we had been close readers of each other's lives, and we knew that we would get a sympathetic and thoughtful hearing if we wanted to talk something through with the other. We had a sense, too, I think, of when the right time was to ask deeply about what was happening in the life of the other. We knew each other down to the hurts and victories of childhood, and we had been fused by painful events: shouting matches between our parents, the fore-closure of the house down the shore, our stepfather's sudden departure and the decision we had reached together to end our mother's care when she had been on life support in a hospital bed. I tended to be more of the talker and prober than Paul, who tended to quietly work things out himself.

There was no doubt: he was emotionally tougher than I was—or maybe he was just more able to carry his pain and problems without expressing them. Our mother had valued this quality of emotional toughness, and encouraged it, and I knew her one concern with me was emotional weakness—my inability to hold up to disappointment in relationships in particular. "Louis, you see the world through rose-colored glasses." Case in point: she had treated the absence of our real father from our lives as a nonevent. It was a fact, and the fact should be treated with indifference. This theme of being strong through tough times was an essential part of her mothering.

I remember a night when I was in high school—I was probably seventeen years old; we had lost the house by then—and we were living in a minimally furnished apartment on the edge of town. There was the usual arguing between my mother and Johnny over his drinking and his inability to hold a job. On this night the shouting intensified, and I heard Johnny say something like, "The hell with this. I'm finished with this shit." He was opening and closing drawers, and I guessed he was throwing clothes in a grocery bag to move out. Listening to their fight from my bedroom, and then hearing the finality of John's statement, made me break down. I began to shake and sob. I went into the bedroom where they had been arguing, and for the first time ever I confronted him. "You can't leave," I said. "You're part of this family." I must have been a sorry sight, shaking and in tears, and they both looked at me with surprise. Their eyes seemed to say, *Why are you so upset?* My shaking left them both silent, and briefly chastened.

My mother wanted her boys to be men. Men were strong. At seventeen I was a man in her eyes. She worried that I lacked the grit to get through the really tough times. Her attitude was rooted in her own experience. Life for her had been a succession of disappointments: being forced to quit high school to work; a first marriage that became almost immediately oppressive and then violent; a second marriage, to a man she deeply loved but who was dissolving in alcoholism; long days and weeks of work in the beauty shop. Life was about survival, and survival meant not giving in to sadness or loss. She kept me close, and I was always her confidant and principal adviser when trouble entered her life, which was often, yet at the same time she feared I would turn into a momma's boy. This was one of the tensions that defined our relationship.

Was I her father or son? As I grew up, I could see she was convinced I would be successful in some profession and bring her honor, and her certitude gave me a powerful confidence outside of our small family unit, but she also thought she was sending a son into the world with a handicap—something, in her mind, akin to a club foot or cleft lip. I lacked her ferocity, and ferocity was necessary to make one's way in the world. As a consequence, I got the attention and praise that is often lavished on a sickly or sensitive child.

Amid the trouble at home, I had escaped to two places—the woods and the library. The loss of the house meant the loss of easy access to the woods, which had been my privilege whenever I wanted it, right out the back door. Once we moved back into town, I spent my entire Saturdays at the Bishop Memorial Library in Toms River. This library, with its big wooden tables, stacks of books and a mezzanine with a milky glass floor, became a second home for me. I sat in a Windsor chair with a small seat pad and wooden arms, from which I read books and magazines as the light shifted sides in the library from morning to late afternoon. The chair itself struck me as representative of a literary life. We had nothing like it at home, and it was better made than anything at school. The library's walls were hung with portraits, landscapes and maps, and its tall windows, which pleasantly framed berry-bearing bushes outdoors, had deep varnished wooden sills upon which I sometimes stacked the books I had gathered for that day's reading. As the hours went by, I would work my way down a pile of six or eight.

I even managed to transform these impulses—for being in the woods and for reading—into the prospect of a career. I decided to become a wildlife biologist and was eventually admitted to the University of New Hampshire's school of forestry. I already had read all of Aldo Leopold and a lot of John Muir and Henry Thoreau and been through every copy of the town library's collection of *Scientific American* magazine. I had a good working knowledge of cell biology.

My commitment to forestry crumbled, however, when I took my first literature class. The English professor introduced me to Emerson, who proved the perfect bridge between my two favorite places, the woods and the library.

I don't know why, but Paul and I didn't talk about the trouble at home when we were growing up. Maybe it was too big a subject for us, or we lacked the words and experience to put what was happening around us into language. We both knew that it was not good, though I suspect we also thought that most people lived this way. Paul seemed less affected by the tumult than I—at least until John left for good, and then it hit him harder. It wasn't until much later, around the time that I separated from my wife and passed through a kind of nervous breakdown, that we began to talk openly about our childhood and what we had made of it. It was a conversation that grew more sustained after our mother died. We both realized, I think, that we had bags to unpack. As we talked, I discovered that we had to some extent experienced different childhoods. Paul had not felt it as a time of anxiety or worry, as I had, nor did he see our mother's life as tragic, as I had viewed it. My guess is that he was closer to the view that she would have expressed herself, a view that would have been shaped by her pride and unwillingness to give in to a sad representation of her life.

To some extent, Paul, I think, shared our mother's view of me as vulnerable. At the same time, I was his older brother, and older brothers almost always come with admiration and standing. I had not been without achievement in the classroom, or courage in the schoolyard. I was not a coward among other boys. Paul looked up to me and was loyal to me in a way that went beyond friendship. These were thick and complicated family ties, and when we became adults the ligaments of mutual support were firmly in place.

We had spent a lot of time together when we built the first house, and we had talked more than we ever had before in our lives. The reliance that I set down on him in the course of that project—he had become the better builder by then—was new to our relationship. Before, I had been the leader, the smart one and the know-it-all. Building the house brought with it challenges that I could not solve without Paul's help, both problem-solving tasks and physical tasks. The shift evened things out between us, and the relationship grew stronger as a result.

Paul's constancy had offered me firm ground through my divorce. He never tired of my taking him through an analysis of the situation that had developed between my wife and me, and he always ended these sessions with the same advice: "Stop beating yourself up." I had also been candid with him about my state of mind when I was first planning the cabin. I told him about the depression that was falling over me, and the visitations of panic and loneliness. "That's not good," he said, and after that he checked on me regularly with phone calls and included me in events at his home with the kids—birthdays, graduations. He had his children call me for advice on their school papers. It all helped.

Now I wanted to help him if he needed it, though it was not

clear whether he did or not. He seemed more relaxed on some days as we worked, but I sensed that he was quietly sorting through a difficult decision.

"If you're needing some money," I told him, "I can help." It was a shot in the dark.

"No," he answered. "I'm fine with money, but thanks."

As we worked on the cabin, I asked him about his job, which he said was going okay, and made small talk about life in general. He said everything was mostly okay but that he was feeling a need to make a change—he wasn't sure what it should be, but there were days when he thought what he really wanted to do was take a year away from everything, get on his bike and drive around the country. "See what's out there," he said. "You know, this life, it isn't a dress rehearsal."

These conversations occurred intermittently as we worked and were interrupted by the need to call out measurements, ask for tools, even make trips to the hardware store, but they unfolded with a steady unity through the day, and sometimes over several days. More than once I heard him use the phrase "not a dress rehearsal."

All through the summer, the hillside was working its magic on me. I was feeling much better. The gloom had lifted, and nature was offering me its cure. Of course, I shouldn't have been surprised. I had counted on it because it had worked for me before.

Where there is harmony there is likely to be health, and what is nature but the harmonious arrangement of air, water, sunshine and soil? I worked hard in the mornings when the day was cool and slowed in the afternoons in the heat. Sometimes, after lunch, I snoozed on the plywood deck, my hat pulled down over my eyes and my sweatshirt rolled under my head as a pillow, and now and again I took a break from my work and walked into the woods nearby to the place where I thought I might plant the orchard. I paced off about an acre, roughly in a square, and surveyed the sun and slope, which seemed to me just right for apple trees. Apple trees like a little slope to shed the cold air that threatens the late frosts of spring; valleys and depressions collect the cold air and are hostile to spring's tender blossoms.

I'm not sure where I picked it up, but I had been carrying around the idea of an orchard of my own for a long time. Everything about an orchard appealed to me: planting and caring for the trees, watching their growth, the ripening toward red and yellow, slipping the slender picking ladder into the branches so I could reach the fruit, the abundance of the harvest and the pies and preserves that would follow.

My favorite food is apple pie and ice cream. I could live on it, I am convinced, and I always feel better after I've eaten a piece. Way back, the apple pie and diner passage in Kerouac's *On the Road* had given me an immediate flash of self-recognition, and later I committed to memory many of Robert Frost's lines about apples. My favorite character in American history is Johnny Appleseed. He is our homegrown John the Baptist, walking west with tattered clothes and a tin pot as a hat, spreading fruit trees and love across the countryside and offering salvation not through water but with a jug of cider. Here was a man who lived the Sermon on the Mount. The old varieties that he had scattered across Pennsylvania, Ohio and Indiana were in themselves a national lyric read aloud—Spys and Winesaps, Pippins, Rhode Island Greenings, Baldwins, Snows and Coppins, Porters, Priestleys and Russets. The names of apples evoke for me our better natures as Americans, and an agrarian past and the sounds of fiddles and dulcimers. Isn't this the country we still wanted it to be? I resolved to plant some of the antique apples in my orchard, should I ever get to put one in. John Chapman of Leominster, Massachusetts, had lived through nature, and nature had lived through him. That was nothing if not harmony.

And what was behind the harmony of the apples, of the pink lady's slippers I found on my farther-ranging walks, or of the yellow mayflies and the trout that sipped them in nearby Great Brook? It seemed to me the result of the inevitable unfolding of laws laid down by the universe and embedded in the elements at hand: air and water, sunshine and earth. It was not by chance that the trees and leaves assumed their unique colors and shapes, or that the small streams flowed into bigger streams, or that the fireflies lit their little lanterns of phosphorescence among the grasses at night. All of this was the consequence of what the universe had commanded. It was chemistry, biology, physics and some inexpressible something else mixed together into one thing, and that thing was inevitability. We respond to the grasses, the trees and the brooks because we sense the deeper truth in them. A brook cannot be false or a tree deceptive, and because we as a species grew up with them, and among them, we are essentially part of them and they of us. By what other means can we be said to be made? What is evolution but the interaction of our potential with the reality of nature? The apples, the leaves, the mayflies, the trout— they express the harmony of nature, as well as the miracle of nature. We are included in this miracle, and the surprise would be that a separation from nature would result in anything *but* alienation from our deepest and earliest selves, that a reconnection would be anything *but* a sense of coming home. All of us, it seems to me, seek to recapture the sensations and selves of our childhoods, and nature offers the best way back, to the freshest parts of our true and original essence.

Spring passed from the hillside. For a week the pine pollen had been so profuse in the air that it left a green skin over the pond's surface. Lilac blossoms had filled the town's dooryards and cemeteries. The nighttime frosts were over. Irises followed the lilacs—wonderfully elegant and purple on their stems, they appeared along the roadsides, in ditches and at the granite foundations of the oldest houses.

We were in the embrace of summer. I spotted a doe in one of the hay fields along the Adams Road. She was as russet as a berry on the bush, and I guessed she was watching over a fawn that she had dropped in the unmowed timothy, hidden from the foxes and coyotes. Fawns are without scent—one of nature's blessings and safeguards. The best part of the day for me was early in the morning when the wood thrushes filled the hillside with their liquid flutelike song. It was as if the pure eight-syllable melody—*tut tup, o-lay-o-lay-o-lee*—were being blown through a water whistle, or had bubbled up from some natural spring. The song was both so pure and so deep—with the notes sounded simultaneously and in a haunting harmony—that it seemed to give dimension to the hillside, defining its boundaries and occupying its hollows. The songs filled the spaces among the trees and rocks as if with colored light, and the final high notes lingered in the cool dappled shade of the oaks and beeches. It was for me the distillate of a woodland summer morning, and it never failed to bring me pleasure.

Even on those days when Paul, Kevin or Billy was unavailable and I worked alone, I was not entirely without company. I was joined by a chipmunk that liked to hop onto the surplus beams we had stacked in front of the cabin, in among the trees. The stack was about four feet high, which seemed to suit my friend. He would climb and sit, working his tail, watch me work for a minute or two, then run off to a pile of rocks in the woods, where I presumed he had a burrow. He was not much bigger than a man's fist, with two white and brown–bordered stripes on his back and shiny black eyes that glowed like tiny spots of wet paint. He was never still, twitching his tail and looking right and left.

For me, a chipmunk was an unusual sight in the Maine woods. I had found red squirrels to be far more common. I accounted for the difference by the abundance of oaks and beeches around the cabin. Red squirrels are pine seed eaters, while chipmunks are more likely to eat nuts. Red squirrels are also noisy scolds and aggressively territorial, and they often make me want to do nothing so much as fire a shot and collect their tails for tying trout flies. Not so chipmunks. This chipmunk seemed to be evaluating my progress with a critical eye. I named him Pericles after the builder of ancient Athens, who I suspect did more supervising than building. Occasionally I'd set out a few peanuts for him. He was oddly selective, taking some and leaving others. We grew used to each other, and he would come close to the deck for a look when some important piece of work was under way. Sometimes when I could not see him, I could hear him (or one of his neighbors, or his Aspasia) issuing a hollow *chuck-chuck* sound framed by sharp clicks. It resounded in the woods like a drummer striking a tom-tom followed by a rim shot. On some afternoons, it seemed like the entire percussion section of an orchestra was warming up around the cabin.

The road I traveled to the cabin each morning took me past the place where the old Adams homestead had stood. It would be hard to imagine a more pleasant setting for a home. There was a gentle swelling of the land, a rising up like a wave at sea, except this wave was grass covered and with a big willow tree near the crest. I guessed the tree must have been dooryard shade at some point in the past, but of course now there was no longer a door nor a yard, though there was a foundation hole lined with rocks and choked with raspberry bushes. The spot offered a lovely prospect, the roll of the meadow, the bend of the tree, the rise and fall of the hills to the west—all of this gave the entire scene a feeling of rhythm and sway. Farther back from the road, to what I assumed would have been the view from the rear of the old house, poplar trees had filled in the meadow and hay fields, and below it to the left—the north—the land sloped toward Cold Brook, which gurgled now as it must have then, cold and clear over smooth stones.

One hundred years ago—even fifty years ago—the land around the homestead would have been open for a half mile or more in every direction before it hit a line of trees, and a person standing in the yard on a summer day like the ones I was experiencing each morning would have seen nearly a dozen other small houses and farms in the intervale and among the cleared hills. Stone walls would have threaded the open land with sheep grazing the grass-

and-rock hillsides. It might as well have been the Cotswolds except for the occasional wolf or moose that wandered down from the north. Back further in time, two hundred years ago, there would have been yet another landscape—dark and unbroken forest except for those places of natural streamside meadows or small patches that had been opened to the light by the earliest settlers, who had come up from the towns around Boston, either directly or by way of Portland or the towns of New Hampshire's Merrimac River valley.

Joseph Adams was one of those early settlers. In 1823, he bought a hundred acres from Mary Batchelder, the widow of Josiah Batchelder of nearby Fryeburg and Boston. Batchelder had received a grant of 28,822 acres from the Massachusetts General Court, for the price of seventeen cents an acre. Batchelder's grant stretched from the New Hampshire border nearly to Kezar Lake. Massachusetts then was still selling its frontier lands to ease its debts, piled up from the Revolutionary War and the War of 1812. Joseph's purchase, which required a mortgage from Mrs. Batchelder, included not only the homestead knoll but my hillside across from the pond. If Joseph followed the pattern of other settlers, he would have cleared the land by first setting fire to it, then pulling the stumps with oxen and chains and lugging the piglet-sized stones that came up out of the ground to piles in his fields, or forming them into the walls that bordered them. The work would have been ferociously hard, and Joseph likely added game to his diet of mutton and beans, corn and root vegetables. There would have been an abundance of bear, deer and even woodland caribou in the vast forest of the north country. He undoubtedly planted apple trees so he would eventually have had cider, and, also no doubt, some of that cider would have been encouraged to ferment so Joseph could enjoy a pleasant buzz as the snow piled high outside his windowsills and he rested his tired bones in front of a blazing fire. Surely some of the gnarled old trees I have encountered in my walks among the hills sprouted from seeds produced by Joseph's trees and carried into the woods in the stomachs of deer and birds.

By 1830, Joseph was married to Mary Robinson. According to census records, there were seven people in his household: Joseph and Mary, and at least four of the others were their children. The identity of the seventh is not clear; perhaps it was a relative who was taken in, or maybe another child. Andrew Jackson was president in 1830, and the tremors that soon would cleave the nation were already being felt. The debate over a state's right to nullify federal law emerged in the Senate that year, and Maine had been admitted to the Union as a free state eight years earlier under a compromise that allowed slavery in Missouri. President Jackson was busy then removing the native peoples from the South—the Choctaw, Cherokee, Creek, Chickasaw and Seminole. The native people who had lived on the land around the Adams homestead— and there had been many—had been killed or driven off seventy-five years earlier.

By the 1830s, Stoneham was a town of subsistence farms and sawmills. There was not a brook in the area that did not have at least one sawmill on it, and its abundance of white and red oak made it a source of staves for the manufacture of wood barrels. Stoneham's staves, the beveled pieces of wood that formed the sides of the barrels, traveled by wagon to Portland and then by schooner to Cuba and the West Indies, where they were assembled into barrels and filled with molasses and rum. The staves were temporarily assembled into barrels in Stoneham to assure their eventual watertightness, and then broken down and packaged into shooks that took up less space in shipping—in the local vernacular, the staves were "all shook up."

There was a sheep and wool boom occurring then, and much of the land in Stoneham and throughout northern New England was sheep pasture. Up to eight thousand sheep a day from Maine, New Hampshire and Vermont arrived at the Boston stockyards, herded along the roads from backcountry farms. The wool was turned into cloth at mills along the major rivers, or at home on spinning wheels.

In 1847, Joseph, then sixty-nine years old, sold his farm to his son William for a thousand dollars and the promise that William would provide "good suitable support" for his father and mother until their deaths. In the 1860 census, Joseph was still alive, at eighty-three, and so was Mary, at eighty. By then they lived with their grandson Joseph Jr., and there were four Adams households in the intervale, probably all of them carved from the original purchase and all of them within a rifle shot of the place where my cabin would eventually be built. In those four households, there were twenty-five people with the surname Adams. In one of those households there were two young Adams brothers—Hosea, fourteen, and Albion, seventeen. They had about the same age spread as Paul and I.

Hosea (as his military record would soon indicate) was five feet, eight inches tall, with dark eyes and dark hair. Albion was taller, a six-footer, with hazel eyes and sandy hair. They lived in the home of Sylvester Adams, another one of Joseph's grandchildren, but they could not have been Sylvester's sons because Sylvester was only thirty years old in 1860. My guess is that they were Sylvester's nephews or cousins and Sylvester had taken them in because a brother or uncle (also in the intervale) had been unable to care for them. The moving around of children among an extended family was not unusual in those days. Families took in other family members' children in hard times. There was no alternative but destitution. Besides, Hosea and Albion would have been welcome hands around Sylvester's farm, strong boys with strong backs. Sylvester appears to have been unmarried at the time, with no children, and he was living with his mother, Sally.

The nullification tremors crested on April 12, 1861. With seven states already having declared their secession from the Union, forces of the breakaway Confederacy attacked U.S. troops at Fort Sumter, South Carolina. President Lincoln called for volunteers to put down the rebellion. Albion enlisted in October 1861. The corn at his uncle's farm would have been harvested by then, and only the gourds would have been left in the stubble fields. When Albion struck off that fall and made his way past Little Pond and the knob and hillside on the way to Norway, and then down to the coast and Cape Elizabeth, where his regiment would muster, the poplar trees would have already turned gold and the bears in the mountains would have been actively foraging in preparation for winter. Maybe one or two would have visited the Adams' chicken house. Surely, the mountain ash was ablaze with its fiery red berries.

Albion's regiment, the 12th Maine Infantry, gathered at Fort Preble on Casco Bay before departing on a steamer for Boston, where it docked briefly, and then embarked on a winter trip to

Ship Island, Mississippi, and then to New Orleans, where it guarded the U.S. mint. Hosea, sixteen, followed his brother into the Union Army in July 1862. Hosea left the farm for Augusta, where his regiment, the 16th Maine, mustered before departing for Washington.

They each got twenty-five dollars, which if combined would have equaled half the value of Sylvester's farm. So maybe they joined for the money, or maybe for the Union cause, or maybe for the adventure, or maybe for all of those reasons. What sort of relationship these brothers had is impossible to know—they have left no discoverable letters or other personal records behind. But for sure they worked closely on the farm as brothers—the work would have taken more than one man, rooting up stumps, hauling rocks from the fields, twitching logs out of the woods. Were they confidants or rivals? Did they argue or cooperate? All I know from the scant records available is that they took the same path away from the farm—there was only one road out of the intervale, and it led past the hillside and the pond—and into the great chasm of civil war.

On the way to New Orleans, a barrel of beef that Albion was loading onto a transport boat rolled and smashed his leg. He was taken out of duty and eventually recovered, though with a cough that had developed while he was recuperating. It steadily worsened and produced blood. Disease took its toll on the Northern boys who came into the South and encountered new germs, and New Orleans—between the malarial mosquitoes and syphilis in the city's numerous whorehouses—extracted a particularly heavy price. Another local boy, also in the 12th Maine, wrote in a letter to a friend:

I have been to as many as a dozen hoar houses and I hant seen but two good stile in the hole lot, but a dirtier damn set of cases you never see. . . . Portland or Boston is a better chance for a good clean time than New Orleans but if you want a Reckless nasty Damn drunken anything of that kind you can get it here.

He noted that seventy-five of his comrades in the regiment suffered the clap. Albion reenlisted but never fully recovered from his bloody cough and was discharged for disability in August 1865. He died at home, most likely Sylvester's home, of a lung hemorrhage, in a bed not more than a quarter mile from the cabin. He would have been twenty-two years old.

Hosea had enlisted with four other young men from town, and fifteen from nearby Lovell. The regiment was drawn mostly from the farm and logging towns of western Maine. It is easy to imagine those men and boys flowing out of the hills onto the dusty winding roads in small but gathering groups until they formed a tattered parade of roughs in gallused trousers, blousy shirts and homemade shoes, shouting "Huzzah and hooray" for the Union. Without much training, the 16th Maine departed for Washington, D.C., and then to the Maryland campaign, which culminated at bloody Antietam (3,650 dead, 17,300 wounded). Then it was on to Burnside's disaster at Fredericksburg, where the general's dithering on the wrong side of the Rappahannock ultimately cost the Union Army a victory against General Lee. On the day of battle, December 13, the Union soldiers—with Hosea and the Stoneham boys of Company D—were lined up against Stonewall Jackson on the Rappahannock Plain just outside of the city. At midmorning, with the fog lifting, the 2nd Division and 16th Maine came under heavy fire and were ordered to charge the Confederate troops. Stonewall Jackson had been patiently waiting for the Union troops to come within range of his artillery. He opened fire. It was an awful, bloody mess, and the Union troops were routed. Hosea was wounded slightly in the battle, but soon returned to service.

Months later, in early May 1863, Hosea experienced another Union debacle, at Chancellorsville. Did Hosea think of the Saco River back home as he crossed the Rappahannock and Rapidan rivers in Virginia on the way to Hooker's defeat in Spotsylvania County? In Stoneham, the brooks and rivers would have been high on their banks and the sucker fish would have been making their way upstream from the lakes. It would have been too early for his uncles and cousins to have planted the first crop of peas in the intervale, but soon, in the woods, the flowers of early spring would make their appearances: blue violet, trillium, blueberry, strawberry, dandelion, meadow rue, jack-in-the-pulpit. Possibly, pleasant memories of the town's woodland scenes gave Hosea comfort in Virginia.

Toward the end of June 1863, a rumor reached the Confederate Army that there were shoes to be had in the town of Gettysburg, in south central Pennsylvania. The Southern army had been fighting in bare feet; a Confederate general sent troops to get the shoes. At the same time, two brigades of Union cavalry had been sent to secure the town. There were other Union troops coming up behind those two cavalry brigades, and among them was the 16th Maine. Neither side expected an encounter, and despite orders from Lee not to engage the enemy before he had pulled together his spread-out army, the Confederate general who had sent for the shoes engaged the Union cavalry. In hours, the most consequential battle of the Civil War was under way. Hosea was in the middle of it.

The Union generals decided to hold their ground at a Lutheran seminary on a small hill west of the town. The Maine boys were positioned behind a rail fence near the seminary, in full view of the enemy two hundred yards away. There was furious firing between the lines, and the Maine regiment was ordered to make a bayonet charge. It drove the Southerners into the woods. The spread-out Confederate Army began to converge on Gettysburg, and it bore down on Seminary Ridge from the north and east. The Union Army retreated, its lines crumbling. The Union command saw that it might save its army if it could slow the Confederate force. The 16th Maine was ordered to remain at the ridge and "hold it at any cost." The mass of Confederate troops fell on the 16th Maine, and soon it was surrounded. The Maine commander broke his sword in the ground, and the men who had not fallen gathered around their regimental flag, refusing to relinquish it to a rebel officer. They tore it and shoved the pieces in their shirts. The men, including Hosea, were taken prisoner. Wounded again, Hosea was held at a Richmond prison and placed in its hospital. He died there on November 5 of typhus.

The war changed the hill country of western Maine. The boys who left to fight saw new lands and places that were easier to farm, with less cruel climates and fewer rocks, and the countryside began to empty out. Farms were abandoned; fields were slowly reclaimed by the forest. In 1860, Stoneham's population was 460. Today it is 255.

The New England landscape that remains a lockbox of America's idea of a virtuous and ideal past—of skating ponds, village churches and flinty but provident family farms—had in fact been in a state of constant change since the arrival of the first Europeans. The end of the great rebellion brought one more change, though it was one from which the region never fully recovered. Gone were the multitude of farms, the small manufacturers, the lively commerce with Europe and the Caribbean, the village life and the steady stream of national leaders.

The question that I pondered as I walked back and forth to the cabin was this: Does the decline of this corner of New England, or at least the disappearance of the old symbols of austerity, self-sustenance and ingenuity that it so firmly embodied, prefigure a decline of the best part of the nation's character? Could I read some warning to America from this little piece of intervale that had so freely given its blood to maintain the Union but had lost its future? Here was the arc: from Eden, to frontier folk, to settled farms, to industrialization and war—and, finally, to long economic decline. Even the wood in the furniture for sale in the big-box stores where local residents pushed their shopping carts was now cut, turned, shaped and glued in Asia. The wood! What happens, I wondered, when a nation loses its work and it becomes a discount shopping mall stuffed with goods manufactured in China?

Sylvester Adams, in whose home Hosea and Albion had grown up before going off to war, eventually married, and he had three sons: Perly, Winfield Scott and John Quincy. John Quincy had a son, Albert, and Albert was the last Adams to live in the intervale. One of my neighbors remembers him sitting on the porch of the house that occupied the knoll. The house and land were sold in

1930 to a rich eccentric from New Jersey, Roy C. Wilhelm, who bought up all the land in and around the intervale during the Depression for a song and raised goats as a hobby. He had been a coffee importer. Wilhelm died in 1951 and left his estate to the National Spiritual Assembly of Baha'i. It was eventually sold off in pieces, the biggest of which went to the developers of the short-lived ski area on Adams Mountain. The hillside piece on which the cabin was rising had three owners between the Baha'i ownership and my purchase, the last before me being R.F. Land Partners, which was Rick Rhea and Wayne Field.

The rain came often in the last two weeks of June, and the mist hovered and moved among the mountains, making them look like steaming teapots. The fields were full of dandelions and yellow and orange Indian paintbrush. The locust trees bloomed, and their pendulous puffy white clusters of fibrous duff made my eyes itch. The pond was swelling with weeds.

I went to the cabin from the inn even when it was raining. I puttered under the plywood roof. I picked up nails and odd board ends on the deck and swept up or straightened out the tools in the toolbox. There was always some little task waiting to be done. I was dry and happy and enjoyed my shelter out of the downpours. Now and again I just stood by the door's rough opening and watched the water come down from the roof and fall from the eaves. Sometimes it came down as drops, one drop following another to form a series of thin watery lines pouring from the roof's edge; other times it was a cascade, something like standing under a paper-thin waterfall. At the roof's valley, where the two roofs met to make an inward crease, the water came down as a spout and sailed into the air as if a cherub were pissing a clear stream from above. Italian Renaissance plazas had nothing on me. So pleasing were these interludes, as the rain fell out of the sky and I stood there shivering with the cold damp air stirring inside my light shirt, that I was convinced they were touching me in some atavistic place. I was in my cave or teepee or hut: like a fox in his den or a raccoon pulled inside a hole in a tree, I was safe and dry. By then, I had a chair in the cabin, and I would just sit and watch the rain come down, tapping the leaves, splattering on the ground or blowing this way and that as the wind shifted.

There are these moments that occur in nature that can stay with a man for a lifetime. Like love, they are almost beyond language. I remember one such experience that was exquisitely distilled into a single spoken word. It taught me that there are subtle pleasures that should not be hurried, and that pleasure itself could bring a man to a higher level of consciousness and leave him with a fuller appreciation of the world he has been born into.

I had traveled to southern Greece years earlier, to the farthest tip of the Peloponnese, and I was staying with a man, deep into his seventies, who was a resident of a mountaintop village there and a relative of mine through my grandmother. He was a gentle and philosophical person, who had lived a life of labor, and now he spent his days gathering herbs, roots and wild vegetables from the hills. His evenings were spent at *kafenios* or quiet *tavernas*, where he talked with his friends long past midnight over water glasses of red wine. He brought me with him on these nights, and afterward we would return to his home—an ancient stone house of one room that looked over the mountains and the sea. One night, he set up two stiff wooden chairs on a small flat space inside

the little compound that was his home. It was a precipitous drop
to the valley of olive trees below; to the right was the Laconic Gulf
and somewhere out there was Kythira, the island to which Paris
had carried Helen on that infamous first night. Straight ahead of
us, as we were seated, were mountains, with a few sparse trees, and
at the ridge of the mountains the moon was rising. It was a big
silvery disc. We had swallowed plenty of wine through the night,
but we were not drunk, and we had eaten well, fresh tomatoes,
feta cheese, crusty bread, olives, fried potatoes, grilled lamb. Stelios, my friend and relative, brought out two cool glasses of water
for us, water he had drawn from his well with a bucket. We
watched the moon ascend and sipped the water. We said nothing.
Stelios spoke no English; I spoke only a little Greek. Slowly, after
several minutes, the big moon cleared the ridge and it was fully
surrounded by the dark Mediterranean sky.

"*Oreia*," Stelios said in Greek. "It's a fine thing."

Yes, I thought, that is the word for this moment: "*Oreia*."

Eventually the rain stopped on the hillside long enough for serious work to resume, and the traffic was heavy, by hillside standards, for the better part of a week. I had hired an excavator to
put in a septic system, having decided that an indoor toilet was
necessary if the cabin were to be a place for family to gather. My
new excavator was Bill Parmenter, from nearby Fryeburg, a neighbor of Billy's. He was seventy-six years old and six feet of sun-
burned sinew—a farmer, builder, excavator and, as I soon learned,
a water diviner. He worked by himself and stopped only at noon
for a few minutes to eat a lunch that was a cellophane packet of
peanut butter crackers. During one of these quick lunches, he

asked me about my well plans, and I told him I hoped to save money by putting in a dug well. I figured on a hole maybe ten to twenty feet deep and lined with a wide cement pipe or stones. I could drop an electric pump to the bottom or rough it with an old-fashioned hand pump. It was standard technology in Stoneham.

"I can help you with that," he said. "I can find the water for you."

"How?" I asked. He was chewing his crackers.

"With a metal rod," he said.

I made my disbelief clear—and showed no deference, as I might have done to local knowledge in other circumstances.

"You're putting me on, right?" I said.

"No. Done it many times," he said.

The next day he was back with a length of steel wire, which he had bent so he could hold the ends lightly in his hands and have it stick out in front of him. He walked through the woods, and sure enough the wire turned and pointed down.

"Water's here," he said.

Yeah, sure, I thought.

"Okay," I said, calling his bluff. "Why don't you dig the well there."

He brought his backhoe into the woods and hit water at five feet, but it was brownish, as if minerals had leached into it.

"I wouldn't use it," he said. "But I knew it was there."

I asked if we should try digging somewhere else. No, he said, this was the only place where his steel wire had told him water was accessible enough for a surface well. So I hired a well driller to give me an artesian well. He arrived in a big truck with a drilling rig that reached nearly to the treetops. For three days the truck roared as the drill rig pounded and turned a bit into the bedrock. It was followed by a pipe casing that eventually would bring water to the surface. At 330 feet deep, the bit found a bedrock fissure with water—two gallons a minute, not a lot but enough to supply the cabin. The bill: $3,400, which was about $3,000 more than I had planned to spend on the dug well.

"Too bad about that," Bill said.

As I considered the siding I wanted for the cabin, I drove around to look at the variety of siding materials and styles on the houses scattered along the town's half dozen roads. I encountered the typical range of housing stock of rural Maine: farmhouses, camps, cottages, log cabins, house trailers, shacks, modular ranches that had been delivered on trucks, chalets, teepees and even a yurt. I paid close attention to the barns, my long-standing fascination, and old public buildings such as the Odd Fellows Hall, the Grange and a wood-framed structure in North Lovell that had been converted into a library. I spent the better part of an hour one morning looking over a vacant wood building that had once been a dry goods store, examining its exterior trim, cornices and lintels. I also found a house, down near Great Brook, that had once been Stoneham's schoolhouse. It had been moved there decades ago from another location in town to be closer to where most of the children lived.

This moving of buildings was common in town in the nineteenth century—people moved houses and barns rather than build new ones, a testament to both their frugality and their skills as builders. The buildings—barns, houses, churches, schools—were moved in winter, typically, when they could be pulled on runners over the snow. Sometimes they were moved for miles. A house or barn moving was a big event, and lots of people turned out for the fun. Long strings of oxen were employed—both ahead of and behind the structure. The animals in front pulled it forward; the animals behind kept it from rushing down the snowy hill. During one move in nearby Lovell, a barn got hung up and blocked the road. The farmer simply opened the doors front and back and let the traffic pass through. There were so many of these movings that I have to wonder if it ever happened that a line of oxen pulling a barn had to stop at an intersection to let another line hauling a house pass by.

My drive-around made it clear that the oldest houses in town were built with the most craftsmanship, and they also seemed to best fit their settings. Of course, this made sense: the best home sites were the first ones taken. I could not help but also notice the decline, over time, in the appearance of the town's housing stock. The successors to the people who had built sturdy, pleasing homes of oak and pine on granite foundations—the same people who had evolved the connected architecture of big house, little house, backhouse and barn—now often occupied factory-built boxes of plastic, vinyl and aluminum. This is an observation, not criticism: my neighbors live in what they can afford, and what is available to them. The story of the deterioration in housing here is one piece, I assume, of the more general slide of the entire nation away from an expectation, regardless of wealth, of craftsmanship and good native materials.

On the older homes, the predominant siding material was clapboards, almost always painted white, and the old seasonal cottages and camps near the lake employed a beveled siding of pine boards, almost always painted green, which appealed to me. It struck me as pleasing, practical and inexpensive. It was this style that I settled on, though I decided I would oil rather than paint them. Paul had recommended a mix of linseed oil and turpentine. It had worked wonders, he said, on preserving wooden ladders.

Billy and I made a trip in his pickup truck to the Lovell Lumber Co., which sawed and milled the siding boards that I liked. It was at the south end of Lovell, on the Kezar River, near the remains of an old water-powered mill. The log yard at Lovell Lumber was piled high with big pine logs that had been cut and hauled from throughout the Saco River valley, which is about as close as one gets to the perfect environment for growing white pine—well-drained sandy gravel soil, adequate rainfall and cold winters. Many of the logs in the yard were three feet in diameter. They smelled of pitch and faintly of licorice, and they made an impressive sight stacked ten and twenty feet high. Still, these logs were pygmies compared to the logs that came from trees that had once grown in this part of Maine. The white pines of the old forest of what is now middle New England were giants. Their bases were bigger around than the columns of the Parthenon, they soared more than two hundred feet into the air and they occurred in stands that would remind us today of the California redwoods. There were other big trees, chestnuts and walnuts, but the most majestic of all were the white pines. A single giant pine would have provided enough wood to build three or four of my cabins. The forest then was a kind of primeval parkland—an Eden for the people who lived there. These people, the Algonquin nations to the south and the Abenaki to the north, were in part responsible for the character of the forest. The history of the forest and the New England landscape was tied up in the customs of the native peoples.

There had been an Abenaki settlement about twenty miles from my hillside until the early 1700s. It was called Pequawket, and it was the picture of small-town life in America for a thousand years before the swarm of Europeans. Of course, America was not yet America then: the people who lived there called it the Dawn Land. A few hundred people, of a group called the Wabanaki, lived at Pequawket in small permanent homes, made of woven sticks and covered with branches and bark. They were farmers as well as fishermen and hunters, and they lived peaceably among themselves, the community governed by consent of the village's residents. They spent their summers, as extended families, at the seacoast. They valued relationships and grieved terribly when a child died, painting themselves black when a death occurred. They abjured wealth, which was a burden to them because it meant weight; and to be fleet was to be free. They liked to move lightly through the forest in their moose-hide moccasins. They had a reverential relationship with the land, believing it was inhabited by spirits. They lived on the land but did not think of themselves as owning the land. They passed a leisurely sort of life, as befit an Eden, which drew on the abundance around them: fish, game, corn, squash, beans, nuts, berries. A Jesuit priest who had observed the native peoples of the region, wrote: "Never had Solomon in his mansion been better regulated and provident with food . . ."

And so the native people lived until (by the European calendar) the late sixteenth and early seventeenth centuries. At about this time, they began dying off in catastrophic numbers from horrific unknown (to them) diseases for which they had no resistance. Typhus, chicken pox, pneumonia, influenza, yellow fever, hepatitis, dysentery, plague, smallpox—the diseases took up to three-fourths of the entire native population. The only explanation the natives had for the deaths was spiritual. Somehow, they had transgressed. Close behind the deaths, like thunder following lightning, came the Europeans themselves, the source of the disease. In the case of the Pequawkets and other tribes of New England, they came as the English, who were building a religious and mercantile colony at Massachusetts Bay. These English people came first to the Indians as traders, seeking furs, especially beaver, which the people of Pequawket were adept at capturing. The commercial engagement with the English was fine with the Pequawkets and the others: they enjoyed the trade and exchanged their furs for tools, cloth, and ultimately guns and alcohol. But later, as the English colony began to outgrow its first perimeters, the English came as settlers, building homes and bringing with them their livestock. The English as permanent residents presented the native people with countless problems. They blocked the streams and their livestock were allowed to wander, playing further havoc with fish-filled waterways and sometimes getting caught in Indian deer traps or causing other mischief. Even the idea of keeping livestock was anathema to the native spiritual beliefs and practices, which bestowed a kind of equality on all forms of life.

Conflicts inevitably arose. The Indians pushed back on the English trespass, and the English returned the push—with force. The English believed they had a right, by God's command, to the wild land. It was improvident to leave these places to the native peoples. It was the Puritan mission to bring civilization in, to clear and cultivate the wilderness and deliver it to their God. To the English, the native people were not fully human, at least not in the way the English themselves were, and this made the taking and killing of them easier.

One incident—of many—captures the English attitude toward the native peoples. In the summer of 1675, a group of Indians traveled down the Saco River to the seacoast—their regular summer trip. They would swim, fish, dig clams and enjoy the cool sea breezes. Near the mouth of the river, they encountered English fishermen. A few of the Englishmen, on seeing the Indians in their canoes, began to speculate on the veracity of a belief among many of the European colonists that an Indian baby could not be made to sink. They laughed and argued about this and decided to make a test. There was an Indian woman in a canoe nearby with her child. Three Englishmen tipped the canoe. The baby sank and died. Now, it happened that this particular baby was the son of the tribe's sachem, Squando. When he learned of his child's death, and its cause, his grief and anger transformed into a rage that was unleashed on English homes and settlers up and down the Maine coast. And so it went. Squando's rage, classical in its proportions and worthy of a treatment by Sophocles, merged with the more general Indian resistance to English encroachment along the Atlantic coast as far south as Rhode Island in a series of deadly clashes called King Philip's War.

By 1690, the Massachusetts General Court was offering a bounty on dead natives. The bounty was collected by bringing scalps to Boston, and Indians who were captured were enslaved, kept by the English colonists or sent to the Caribbean for sale.

Indian genocide by our religious forebears proceeded relentlessly through the seventeenth and early eighteenth centuries. Within biking distance of the cabin was a trace of this most shameful aspect of the nation's history. In 1725, a group of Massachusetts men, led by a roughneck named John Lovell, traveled to Pequawket to kill Indians and collect scalps. They ambushed a group—men, women and children—and a battle ensued that ended pretty much in a draw. Lovell and some of his comrades (including a Harvard divinity student) were killed, but most of them escaped back to Boston, where they were regarded as heroes. In time, these men and their relatives were granted ownership of a big tract of land just north of Pequawket in recognition of their horrible deeds. That tract of land is now the town of Lovell, Maine. I buy my wine there at the Center Lovell Market. The site of what was once Pequawket is the grounds of an annual agriculture fair in the town of Fryeburg, and adjacent to the fairgrounds is Fryeburg Academy, which received a grant of land from the Massachusetts General Court in 1796 in appreciation of the early men of the region who cleaned out the "savage nation."

By the middle of the 1700s, prior to the American Revolution, the Wabanaki were cleansed from the countryside. Nearly all of those who had survived retreated to St. Francis, Quebec, on the St. Lawrence River, where another bully by the name of Robert Rodgers took a group of English colonists and burned the village and slaughtered its inhabitants in 1749. These men were also rewarded with big tracts of land around Pequawket. All this is terribly ironical now. Beset as we now are by problems of pollution, global warming, diminishing natural resources and alienation from our environment, we can see that the native peoples offered a lesson in sustainable living and a reverence for God's creation—one that would serve us well today. Theirs is a history worth recovering and celebrating.

But to bring this back to my siding and the white pine I was buying at Lovell Lumber: the native people not only were farmers, hunters and fishermen; they were also foresters. Their tool was fire, and they used it prodigiously. They burned the underbrush regularly to make travel and hunting easier and to encourage the growth of trees that they favored, especially nut-bearing trees. The forest of middle New England before the arrival of the Europeans was a magnificent garden of giant trees—chestnut, oak, hickory and beech—which mostly covered the upland areas. But none of these came close to the size of the monumental pines, which would tower over them by fifty feet. Those great white pines are long gone. You might as well look for a wooly mammoth.

The elimination of the natives was followed by the stripping of the forest. It was cleared for lumber and then used as farmland or sheep pasture. Hillsides were left bare, and billions of board feet of logs were floated down the region's rivers to sawmills. The logs were turned into lumber and the lumber into houses and cash. A lot of it was shipped to the sugar plantations of the Caribbean. It wasn't until the widespread abandonment of Maine farms following the Civil War that a new crop of pine trees emerged on the fallow landscape. The old titans had grown mostly along the rivers, where they were protected from the wind by ridges that followed the watercourses. The logs that I was admiring in the yard at Lovell Lumber were part of the new succession of Maine pine that had grown up on the stone wall–threaded uplands that had once been farms.

*　　　*　　　*

The drop siding that Billy and I brought back from the lumberyard went up slowly, one board at a time. There was no rushing
it. It looked good, but it was a task that required two men working methodically to accomplish. The upper edge of the boards was
square with a groove; the lower edge had a cove that beveled into
a tongue. The tongue of the board above fit into the groove of the
board below. This created a tight seal against the weather. The
challenge was fitting tongues into grooves over long spans. Sometimes we could just pound the upper piece down into the lower
piece, but more often than not the upper piece needed to be
worked in by putting a wedge behind the upper piece to help it
find the groove of the lower piece. We began at the bottom of each
wall of the cabin and stepped our way up to the top.

The wood was a buttery white and yellow and smooth to the
hand. The long pieces flexed if turned flat to the earth and sky,
and were stiff if turned with their edges down. At the mill, pine
boards had come in several grades depending on the clarity of the
wood, meaning the absence of knots, which are the vestiges of
branches growing out of the tree's trunk. I had bought a grade
that was run-of-the-mill, meaning we encountered a fair number
of red and occasionally black knots. Red knots were fine; black
knots tended to fall out of the board. We trimmed the boards to
eliminate big or troublesome knots and found that we had very
little waste. The drop siding had been a good choice. It gave the
cabin a finished but unfussy look.

I liked the idea of using local wood to build the cabin. There
was a harmony and rightness to it. My wood wasn't coming from
Ecuador's rain forests or Siberian clear-cuts. It came from the

sandy loam soils of the watershed of which the cabin and I were now a part, and I was feeling very good about it. The owner of the sawmill had told me that the valley could continue to produce pine and his mill could continue to saw it into perpetuity with wise management of the resource. This also seemed a good thing. If a man knew and cared about the source of his lumber, just as if he knew and cared about the source of his food, wouldn't it necessarily follow that a lot of mischief and wickedness would be avoided?

The feeling was real, and the question legitimate, but the ideal as it turned out was an illusion. I did a little checking on the origins of the other materials for the cabin. The gaslights I intended to install came from China—I could only guess under what conditions the Chinese workers had labored to produce them. The nails, manufactured by a Japanese conglomerate, came from China. The Japanese conglomerate owned a North American subsidiary, based in New York, which manufactured the nails in China and distributed them in the United States through another subsidiary, in Irving, Texas. The Chinese factory, I determined, was probably in Qingdao, on the north Chinese coast, and employed peasants who had recently migrated from the countryside and received the equivalent of about three hundred dollars per month. They were good nails, and inexpensive. They came in a thirty-pound bucket that cost $30.14 at my lumberyard, which was about two cents a nail. I used two buckets.

The cabin would be made mostly from Maine wood, but it was not in the end an organic loaf made from local yeast and grain. There was too much progress to be gained, and money to be saved, by accepting the benefits of technology and global trade.

For a cabin builder, this was a conundrum not easily solved. How might the balance be struck between the availability of low-price products whose provenance was unknown to me, on one hand, and social and environmental responsibility on the other? Was this balance something that could legitimately be delegated to government through regulation? For example, might the government forbid importation of nails or gaslights produced under inhumane or planet-damaging circumstances? Or must I investigate the sources of all the materials I used to determine their suitability and alignment with the ethical standards I subscribe to? There were no local sources for many of the items I needed. Are nails still mass-produced in the United States? I did not find them. Yet surely the use of a product made by slave labor or through the addition of toxic chemicals or processes implicates me in a crime.

No product more exemplified my inability and unwillingness to escape modernity than the rubbery material I would apply to the sheathing to prevent leaks in the cabin's roof—something called Ice & Water Shield, which is manufactured by W. R. Grace & Co. Stoneham is metal-roof country. Through the trees, a driver often sees glints of silver that could be mistaken for ponds. They are in fact metal roofs. There is the occasional asphalt shingle roof, but mountain winters have schooled local people in more serious overhead protection, and the material of choice is steel. It used to be that they were uniformly silver, and many were the old tin roofs typically found on Quonset huts, chicken coops and third-world shanties. They now come in green, several shades of blue (including an electric blue) and red. Nearly all of these roofs have one thing in common: the dermis below the steel is Ice &

Water Shield. It is stickier than flypaper and difficult to apply, and after my experience with it I named it Ice & Water Torture. But it is supremely effective. Nearly everyone in the hill country uses it because it so completely keeps water on the weather side of the sheathing.

Ice & Water Shield is made at plants in Chicago and Mt. Pleasant, Tennessee. Its ingredients are oil, asphalt, rubber, polyethylene and paper. According to Grace, the oil comes from a refinery in New Jersey, the asphalt comes from Illinois, the polyethylene from Texas, the paper from Finland and the rubber from Mexico. What is a cabin builder to do? I bowed to the prospect of dry ceilings and used Ice & Water Shield—many, many rolls of it. It is difficult to leave the world behind.

By the end of July, the cabin had a roof. The son of Bill Parmenter, my water wizard, installed it for me. He had the skills and specialized tools for bending and cutting metal, and I did not. The roof's green metal surface warmed and shined in the sun. It was the green that I associated with Adirondack pulling boats, Maine warden camps and old spruce trees, demonstrating once again that I was both making shelter and trying to write a poem.

Paul had enlisted a plumber friend of his from Portland, who installed a reserve tank in the loft above the bathroom. It would hold water pumped in through a long blue plastic pipe from the well. Smaller black plastic pipes would carry the water down to sinks in the kitchen and bathroom, to a shower and, most impressively, a bathtub. Paul had retrieved a giant iron claw-foot tub that had been pushed aside in the basement of his church. It was dirty and chipped but it was huge, a Halifax dory of a bathtub. I liked the idea of soaking in hot water after a day of snowshoeing, so I set about restoring it. I scrubbed and sanded it, then washed it with an acid solution and painted it white. It looked as new as the day it passed out of the foundry in Portland in 1898. This would be the cabin's touch of luxury.

The next step for us was the installation of the windows. A double-hung window is an ingenious device, and a world of its own inside the universe of carpentry. There is the window frame, which is made up of jambs (the side walls), a header (the top) and a sill (the base). Inside this frame are set two sashes (windows)— one up and one down. An elegant but strong crosshatching of millwork called muntins divides each sash into numerous lights (or panes). The sashes ride between interior and exterior stops, and between them is a so-called parting strip (or bead). This allows the sashes to move up and down as needed, without rubbing against each other. In a double-hung window frame, four pulleys are set into the jambs, through which ropes are attached to window weights. The ropes ease the opening and closing of the sashes and stabilize them in a fixed position.

I was proud of my windows, with their multiple panes crosshatched into ten over ten and ten over eight. They would give the cabin a distinctive traditional appearance and admit generous quantities of light. At the moment, with the window openings roughed out but no windows installed, the cabin looked like a man without his dentures. But getting the windows ready for installation was going to take some clever retrofitting. We had to make new parting strips and stops because the old ones were damaged. Paul made them from leftover pine stock. Since we didn't have any of the old windows' exterior trim, we were confounded by the problem of fitting the windows to new trim. The original trim had been milled with channels that slipped onto the original jambs, making a tight seal. Paul solved the problem by running the new trim over the blade of the table saw several times to create a dado (or groove) that accepted the old jamb. It worked perfectly.

A cabin without a porch is a lesser creation. It is a hat without a brim, a boat without a prow, brandy without a cigar. My plan was to put the porch in the cavity we had created when we thrust the ell forward from the front of the cabin. There was a full fourteen feet from the inside wall of the ell to the corner of the cabin. If the forward edge of the porch finished even with the front of the ell, which it should for a pleasing appearance, I would gain a porch with dimensions of fourteen feet by ten feet. It was plenty of porch, creating enough space to accommodate four Adirondack chairs or a card table and four folding chairs or four cords of wood, plus a path to the door. In cinematic terms, it was just enough space for Fred to spin Ginger, but not quite enough, as the old saying goes, to swing a dead cat. I also wanted it screened against bugs. With a depth of ten feet, we would have to pitch its roof less steeply than the main roof of the cabin; otherwise, the roof would come down at about five feet at the front edge of the porch, the height of my Adam's apple. Reducing the pitch had a big drawback. Snow was less likely to shed of its own accord from the metal surface. It would need to be pulled or shoveled off a couple of times a year. There was nothing to be done about it. We needed the height to make the porch work, so the pitch would have to be diminished. Could I have avoided this? I guess I could have pitched the entire roof less steeply but still made it steep enough to let gravity do its work with the snow. I could have also raised the top plate of the wall. I ran those cabin profiles through my mind and liked neither of them. Our plan had been sound. I would just buy a roof rake and brace the porch's roof against the eventuality of me failing to get up some weekend after a giant snowfall. It would be fine.

I had to break my summer work for a trip to New York. I dragged myself back into the world, and Paul took on the task of building the porch. I returned and was surprised to find that he had it fairly well completed. He had finished the floor framing and the rafters, and all that remained was for us to sheathe the porch roof and eventually put up the rail and balusters.

By now in mid-August, the pond was as thick as vegetable stew, and showy white water lilies floated on the surface. They were as big as salad bowls in the mornings; toward evening they shrank to teacups. I saw daily blooms of darning needles, those iridescent blue dragonflies that manage to hover and dart with astonishing speed, whirring their four transparent wings. No doubt they came from the pond, where they had lived as nymphs in the mud. Maybe it was the plethora of these bejeweled and delicate insects that accounted for the absence of mosquitoes that we enjoyed at the cabin. Darning needles are great eaters of mosquito larvae.

This was a period of frequent thunderstorms. Often, as I drove to the hardware store or Melby's, the National Weather Service would break in to the radio program I was listening to, with static and an alarmed voice warning of severe thunderstorms, which were great fun when they broke over the hillside with fierce cracks and booms and buckets of water falling from the sky. Standing out in one for just a minute left you as soaked as if you had gone for a swim. In hardly any time, though, the sun would be out again, the leaves sparkling and the blue darning needles darting this way and that over the wet ground. Even as the clouds disappeared and the thunder booms traveled ever farther away, the air remained suffused with moisture and smelled of sulfur, and the humidity lingered into the nights, which now were beginning to cool. The late summer nights carried the scent of cut hay and overripe vegetation. The season was fading.

This was the time when the birds began to congregate in readiness for their flights south. The pond was a resting place and feeding station for migratory birds. Some of the migrations were already under way. The teal, bluish buzz bombs, were the first travelers to arrive and then depart. The wood ducks departed soon after. They were spring and summer residents, and each male wood duck was a glorious sight as it exploded from a woodland stream, offering only the quickest glimpse of its red head, cinnamon breast and lemon yellow flanks. I walked to the pond's far side, passing through the woods and meadows that rimmed it to reach its outlet. A small brook flowed over and through a derelict beaver dam and carved a muddy channel through a boggy place spiked with gray tree trunks, remnants of the flood from an earlier dam that must have increased the circumference of the pond and killed the surrounding timber.

The mud at the outlet was rich with insects, and scores of goldfinches were provisioning against the long flight ahead. They were late nesters and would be among the last to depart the pond and hillside. I scanned the pond's edges for the great blue herons and snowy egrets I had seen in the summer. The egrets reminded me of those old-fashioned carpenter's rulers that were a half dozen pieces of pinioned wood that could fold to fit into your hand or extend up to six feet in length, depending on the need. I saw neither herons nor egrets, and I guessed both were standing in the warm water of a Caribbean cay, maybe picking up shrimp. Ah, Maine to the West Indies! The great coastal sweep from the Maritimes to Martinique was not a watershed, but it was a coherence of natural order, made so by winds, currents, weather and wildlife. Was there a better place on earth than this magnificent littoral? If so, I hadn't yet seen it. I was lost in one of my Atlantic meditations when I heard the scratchy and guttural *yawk* of a raven. I looked up and saw it perched on the limb of a big hemlock tree. He was no migrant or fair-weather resident. He and I would share the hillside through the winter.

We continued to work at the cabin on weekends, and in October we put down the floor. I had bought pine boards, ten inches wide, from Lovell Lumber. They were square edged and straight and fit nicely together side by side. When a gap appeared between two boards, we bent the next board tightly into place, using a crowbar as a lever. We drilled shallow holes at the positions where we set the screws to secure the pine boards to the subfloor. This allowed us to countersink the screws, which eventually I would plug with oak pegs. It would be a handsome floor once it was finished. Already, its smooth buttermilk surface transformed the cabin, making it into an almost finished living space. It invited a walk around in just socks. And that is just what I did—I walked around in my wool socks, feeling it underfoot, and then I skated around on the smooth planed surface. I placed a camera on an empty box at the far end of the cabin, turned on the automatic shutter and kneeled on one knee next to Paul at the other end to record our achievement.

The month closed with reds and yellows on the hillside. It had been almost exactly a year earlier that we made our first failed attempt at the foundation. Now the completion of the cabin was within sight.

CHAPTER 8

RESPONSIBILITIES

In the twenty-two years that I was married and living in Maine, from 1974 to 1996, I built a house, a career and a professional reputation. I had moved from being the most junior reporter at the newspaper in Portland to its editor in chief. My life in those years had been a steady professional ascent. I was not famous, but I became a substantial person in my field. I worked hard, stayed late and went into the office on weekends. I was invited onto the boards of community organizations and asked to make speeches. I took my family on vacations to Florida, put my children through private schools and owned a sailboat. I bought my wife a piano and my daughter a horse, and I took my son fishing in Canada. I made an identity as a husband, father and editor. Eventually, it all came undone.

In 1995, the year before I left Maine for Philadelphia and separated from my wife, I would drop by my mother's apartment two or three times a week in the evenings after work. She looked forward to my visits and made dinners for me. I would sit and watch television or read a magazine while she cooked, and then she would serve me, and we would eat together and talk. I was fortunate then to be earning enough money, as editor of the newspaper, to pay her rent and help her in other small ways. After our dinners, I took her for short walks in the neighborhood to keep her moving and mobile. She held my arm and shuffled along.

By then, I was deeply lonely in my marriage, and these evenings with her provided me with some relief from the silence and tension at home. I said a little about the situation to her, but never fully divulged the scope of my despair. She listened. Things would work out, she told me. Things always happen for a reason, she said. It had been her life's philosophy: *Que será, será*—what will be, will be. In these, the final years of her life, I think she was worried about me, as she always had been, but she also was content in her own life. She had her two sons and her grandchildren nearby, a nice apartment, a small circle of friends at church, and she was retired. It was no longer necessary, after fifty years as a beautician, for her to stand on her feet all day long to cut, wash and color people's hair.

My decision to move to Philadelphia shook her. She never asked me not to move, but I saw the flinch when I made the announcement to her. Even in my forties, I was still her good boy. She knew that my moving meant I would not be coming by for dinners or evening walks and she would see me only occasionally, maybe a few times a year.

She was seventy-three years old then, and it may have been only a coincidence that her decline became more rapid with my departure. She needed a lot of attention. The swelling in her legs grew severe, and her breathing was labored even when she moved short distances. She developed a severe hernia, and because of her overall poor health her doctor advised against surgery. So she lived with it, and the disfiguring presence of it. Soon she needed a walker. Paul was right there in Portland, and he took on the cease-less work of looking after her.

The first crisis came when Paul was forced to take away her car. She loved the freedom it gave her, but her driving was a danger to herself and others. Paul kept her car parked in a place where she could see it from her apartment window, but he took the keys and disabled the battery. Then her memory began to slip. She started to forget small things at first, like the days of the week, and then bigger things, like turning off the kitchen stove. One night, she left a burner on and a dishtowel caught fire. No serious dam-age was done, but it was clear that she could no longer live by herself. It fell to Paul to have the face-to-face conversation with her that it was time for her to leave her apartment and move into a senior housing complex where her meals would be served in a common dining room. She would lose her kitchen. Paul searched for a facility, found the right one and persuaded her to move in. He brought our uncles into the transition, and together they paid her new and much higher rent.

My divorce was then under way. The cost of it meant I was no longer able to send my mother checks for her rent. I was sick about it; I had resolved long ago to provide for my mother in her old age. When my marriage came apart, I came apart too. The mar-riage had been my bulwark against the demons of my childhood—instability, loneliness, fear of abandonment. When the bulwark collapsed, the first thing to go was my confidence. I was unable to make decisions about most anything. I then lost my ability to concentrate—not an insignificant problem as I was just beginning a new job. I was overwhelmed with a general anxiety that came into focus as a feeling that I was spinning downward, toward a life that had no meaning and would end in complete aloneness. None of this made any sense nor could it be justified rationally—it was craziness, pure and simple—but it felt real enough to put me in the hospital with my first episode of atrial fibrillation. That stay lasted seven days at Hahnemann Hospital in center city Philadelphia. The doctors shocked my heart back into a regular rhythm with two paddles while I was under general anesthesia. I left the hospital with singed chest hairs and a three-month supply of blood thinner.

I relate all of this because it explains how little help I was to Paul through the crisis of our mother's decline. The good son had collapsed in a divorce. Paul had stepped forward and took on all of the responsibilities of being a good son. He had become the reliable one—the one to call when there was a problem.

The demands that our mother's health put on Paul multiplied over the next few years. He drove her to doctors' appointments two or three times a week, picked up her prescriptions and organized her medicines in a plastic box with day-by-day compartments. He checked on her daily to make sure she was taking the medicines. Often she did not. As he was attending to her needs, he was working at his job and helping his new wife in her restaurant. Through this whirlwind, he also regularly brought his children to our mother's tiny apartment for visits in the senior housing complex, and he dealt with her growing number of complaints. She was getting more cantankerous as she aged. The two of them bickered and argued—just as they had in the old days, except now it was over her health and unwillingness to follow the doctor's instructions or the rules of her new home. She was as fierce as ever, and Paul could be his rough self too. Sometimes they wouldn't speak to each other for a few days, but they always eventually resumed where they had left off—Paul insisting that she obey the doctor's prohibition against eating candy, or she telling Paul not to order her around.

As for me, I called her nearly every day from Philadelphia to check in, and she talked about the children, events at her church, a recipe she wanted to prepare or a food show she had seen on television. She often praised Paul, "I have to hand it to that brother of yours," she said. "I couldn't get by without him." There were no references, direct or indirect, to his being the bad boy anymore. She would occasionally say, "He can be awfully gruff," and as I listened to her I would think to myself, *Under the circumstances, he's entitled to be a little gruff.* When I visited Paul on holidays and asked him how Mom was doing, he would just roll his eyes. It told me everything I needed to know about the two of them. I had seen it all before.

She went from a walker to a wheelchair, her hair had thinned considerably and fluid oozed from her legs when they swelled. Her feet ballooned and were as puffy as pink foam slippers. She had lived her entire life with a single functioning kidney, and that lone organ now was insufficient to the demands that were being put on it. She required heavy elastic stockings to compress her legs, and either Paul or his children would sit on the floor in front of her and do the work of putting them on or taking them off. She was unpredictably flatulent then. If their help with those elastic stockings wasn't a demonstration of love, I don't know what is.

One night I got a call from Paul telling me that she had gotten the flu, and it was bad enough, in the context of all her other problems, that she needed to be hospitalized. My heart froze. Had the end arrived? I said I would immediately come back to Maine. He said I could wait if I wanted to, and he would let me know if the situation worsened. His voice was subdued, and it seemed to come from a place very far away. "No," I said. "I'm on my way."

The flu came under control, but something worse happened: she picked up an infection in the hospital. She already had it when I arrived the next day from Philadelphia. It had begun as a fever. Its source was a virulent strain of hospital bacteria, and soon it raged through her body. Her temperature spiked and she lost consciousness. Let this stand as a definition of irony: she picked up the illness that would kill her in the place she had gone to be healed. Maybe a doctor had neglected to wash his hands. Maybe a nurse had forgotten to sterilize an instrument. It's impossible to know. No one at the hospital was in a big hurry to find out.

Paul and I stayed at the hospital around the clock during the six days she struggled against fever and failing organs. We slept on the floor of the waiting room. The many ailments that had conspired decades ago to swell her body finally had converged and undercut her ability to fight the infection. She did not let go easily. She had always plunged into life, often recklessly, and now she was clinging to it tenaciously between the stainless steel rails of her hospital bed. Even with her gut ravaged by some implacable microbe, she wasn't willing to leave this world without a battle. With the help of machines she had fought death to a stalemate. At one point, swollen from the liquids that had been pumped into her to maintain her blood pressure, which had dropped precipitously, she regained consciousness for a few seconds. Weakly she asked me, "Louis, am I going to die?" I said, "No, Mom. Hold on." So my last conversation with my mother contained a lie: let this stand as a second definition of irony. Her kidney failed, and the antibiotics dripping into her arm through an IV tube were powerless to suppress the infection. Two days later, a young doctor, a woman with a long white coat, clipboard and crisp professional manner, took Paul and me into a waiting room and said the situation was hopeless.

"I would like your permission to withdraw support," she said.

"What will happen if we don't?" either Paul or I asked.

"We will continue to keep her alive, but I don't think she will recover. The chance is very slight, perhaps one or two percent. We will have to put her through a lot of pain to try to get to that point. If she does recover, her life afterward will not be good. She will spend a lot of time in the hospital. She will not go back to her life as it was. The infection is far too severe. Essentially, she has no intestine left."

We asked more questions, talked between ourselves, wept, called the doctor back into the room and gave consent to withdraw care. We must have signed papers, but I can't recall. We were with my mother when her death came later that day. Her breathing slowed over the course of several minutes, and then it stopped. A respectful nurse turned off the monitor over her bed. Paul made the funeral arrangements. His two daughters went to the funeral home and fixed her hair and applied her makeup. The church was full. My daughter sang "Amazing Grace." I gave the eulogy.

CHAPTER 9

THANKSGIVING

It was a good acorn crop that year. They began falling from the red oaks around the cabin in October. On some days, there was the steady sound of them hitting the ground. *Thunk, thunk.* Pause. *Thunk.* The acorn of the red oak contains more tannin than that of the white oak, sharpening the bitter taste, but still a good crop of nuts from these oaks was a blessing for the deer and grouse and even my little friend Pericles. I hoped he was okay. I had not seen him in weeks. Each acorn would have been an armful for him. He would be well provisioned for winter under the rocks by the porch that Billy was sure was an Indian burial mound.

Toward the end of October, Paul and I set a goal for ourselves. We wanted to have Thanksgiving dinner at the cabin. Actually, it was Paul who suggested it. The thought of it had crossed my mind, but I figured it was too ambitious for me to ask of him. But with the mention of it coming first from him, I agreed it would be an awfully good thing and said we should try to make it happen. Paul was famous in the family for preparing big Thanksgiving dinners. He combined traditional dishes with some of our mother's favorite concoctions—stuffed grape leaves, lasagna, spanakopita and her signature cranberry relish made with walnuts and oranges and a freight-car-load of sugar.

We still had a lot of work to do inside the cabin, some cosmetic, some essential. The interior window trim needed completion and painting. The plumbing was still not hooked up, and in fact we still didn't have water to the cabin. There was not yet a woodstove for heat or even a stovepipe through the roof. The nights and some of the days were cool now, even cold, and heat would be necessary if we were going to bring people for dinner. The wall between the kitchen and the bathroom was still bare studs. We had to put up Sheetrock to make them separate rooms. There was also the matter of the electrical wiring. The cabin would not be connected to the power line down at the road, so I needed to bring electricity from the outdoor generator (also not yet in place) to the cabin and the well pump in the ground for running water. Paul had the name of an electrician who could help us with the wiring. We would do the grunt work of pulling wire through the studs and outdoor conduit, and the electrician would handle the panel and the connections to the devices.

To get all of this work done, we had to step up the pace. We were speeding along one day, working overhead filling in some of the blank spaces in the ceiling boards, when Paul smacked his thumbnail hard with the hammer. It immediately turned purple and throbbed as the blood from the bruise pushed up the nail. He applied pressure on it to slow the pooling of the blood, but the pain was bad enough to make working difficult. He kept going, but I could see he was having trouble. So I proposed a solution I had learned on a construction job and had once used on myself:

piercing the thumbnail to relieve the pressure. It would hurt a bit at first, I told him, but it would then feel immediately better. He agreed. I sterilized a tiny drill bit with the flame of a butane lighter and went to work in my operating room—the front seat of his truck. Slowly and carefully, I turned a tiny drill bit, about an eighth of an inch in diameter, back and forth with my thumb and forefinger over Paul's thumbnail to make a hole. "You're going to know it when I touch the flesh," I told him. "That's okay," he said. "It can't be any worse than what I'm feeling right now." The bit came through and the pressurized blood shot over the dashboard and onto the windshield. He wrapped his thumb with a handkerchief and tied it tight.

We installed the trim around the inside of the windows. I had picked a bright red paint for the trim to give the place a cheerful look. The paint store called it tomato red. To me, it looked more like cream of tomato red. This was another controversial decision. Kevin did not approve. "You're going gay, Uncle Louie." He favored a dark green, and I saw that Paul was in silent agreement with him. Green was the standard move—the traditional choice. I held firm to the red. A little touch of the fanciful couldn't hurt, and in the dead of winter, when the days were cold and short, it might do a world of good to enter a cabin with some bright colors. Kevin came around, but then I took a step too far. I picked pumpkin as the color for the trim in the bathroom. To my team, the choice was incomprehensible. Pumpkin? Again, I held firm. Pumpkin was one of my two favorite pies. I would soak in the tub and meditate on pumpkin.

Near the end of October, I got some very good news. My son, Adam, was returning from Peru for a brief trip to the United

States I would have his company for a few days. He would visit me, his mother in New Hampshire, and several parishes and college campuses in New England as part of his work for the church. He had entered a Catholic religious order based in Peru soon after college and had been in continuous formation and training since then. I had not seen him since the previous year when I had traveled to Lima and together we'd prepared a Thanksgiving dinner for his community of brothers and aspirants. I had missed his companionship these last few years. His absence had knocked a big hole in my life.

Adam had been my closest fishing partner when he was a boy, and since he had been away I had mostly lost the urge to take my fly rod down to the brooks. Fishing by myself held little interest for me. An awful lot of the enjoyment I had gotten from fishing during his boyhood, I had come to see, had derived from being able to introduce him to the wonders of the streams and woods as I knew them—how to read the water, how to identify insects and match them with our homemade trout flies, how to induce a fish to strike, how to release a fish so it survived. He had been a good student. Without him to take along, I didn't feel the same excitement about getting out to the stream. Here's another thing we learn as we get older: sharing a pleasure magnifies it.

After he had gone to Peru, Adam would write to me from time to time of mission trips to the Sierra highlands, and he included details of the streams, insects and fish. I replied with regular updates on the cabin. It was a treat for me now to have him home, even if he could not stay long enough to be with us at Thanksgiving. At the cabin, we painted window trim together, ate a big dinner at Melby's and spent the night at the inn before returning to Boston the next day, but not before I had taken a moment to show him Great Brook, which, I told him, held some nice-sized wild trout. We agreed that one day we would fish it together. I hoped that day would come.

Paul and I gained ground, and Thanksgiving in the cabin seemed attainable. We built a platform for the generator, which Paul hauled up in his truck, and we slid it—all five or six hundred pounds of it—into place. *Bam!* On that day, in the second week of November, I saw the first skim of ice on the pond and ice crystals on the damp leaves. The maples were now bereft of all foliage. Responding to pressure from Paul, the electrician showed up the weekend before Thanksgiving, and so did Paul's friend Steve, the plumber. There's nothing like having a couple of competent men on the job who really know their trades. They worked along steadily, and soon we had both power and water. Russell came up another day with Paul, and the two of them put a shed around the generator to protect it from the weather and muffle the noise when it was turned on to power the well pump. I had forgotten to get a building permit for the shed. I bought the permit after it was up and paid the fine.

Throughout the month, I had gone back to the online classifieds in search of a heavy-duty, airtight and inexpensive woodstove. Either they were cheap or they were well built but never both cheap and well built. I was hanging tough, though, and waiting for my Scandinavian cast-iron dream to show up for three hundred dollars or less. The heating season had already begun, and I was sure that the demand for secondhand stoves had slackened. Some seller would weaken and prices would drop if I could be patient. In the meantime, Russell produced a box stove from his barn that would get us through Thanksgiving. Of course, it required a stovepipe to vent the smoke out of the cabin.

Paul and I wrestled with it for half a day trying to get it right. The challenge was to bring the pipe from the stove to the hole in the roof. It was not a straight shot. The pipe came in two-foot sections, and any turn required a prefabricated elbow with a limited range of flex. The pipe's trip from the stove through the roof involved two elbows, neither of which had a simple ninety-degree angle, and a final piece of pipe that had to be trimmed short of its full two feet to make it fit the length. The entire span of pipe, from stove to roof, was about sixteen feet, which also meant that we would need to hang wires from the ceiling to support the pipe's weight. We did all of this work, on ladders no less, but not without my resolving never to install another stovepipe ever again.

At about this time, a most astonishing thing happened. Actually, it was two astonishing things, and they converged on the memory of John Kababick. One of his sisters, in her sixties— someone I had last seen about forty years earlier, when I was a teenager and she was in her twenties—had tracked me down and sent me a warm and thoughtful e-mail. I remembered her as a young woman in nursing school, the youngest of Johnny's three sisters. Over a period of months we exchanged e-mails and we talked on the telephone, revisiting some memories, both good and painful. In one of our last conversations, she told me she had found a tackle box with a collection of Johnny's fishing lures that he had used as a boy and young man. She asked if I would like to have them.

They came as a gift in the mail, and they left me speechless. I opened the box and just sat with it for a while. I felt the loss of him all over again. Paul and I carried vivid and powerful memories of Johnny, but we rarely spoke of him. There seemed not much more for us to say, or to know. The verdict had been in for a long time. But the emergence of his sister and then of the fishing lures stirred the sediments of our past. There were six fishing lures that arrived, carefully wrapped in a box. With the lures was his seaman's identification card:

> JOHN W. KABABICK
> DATE OF BIRTH: 3-1-30
> ABLE SEAMAN
> HEIGHT: 6-0
> WEIGHT: 220
> COMPLEXION: RUDDY
> EYES: BLUE

There he was in the photo—much older than I had remembered him, but still with his open face and the slightly crooked nose that had been broken while he was the navy's heavyweight boxing champion of the Pacific fleet. His mouth was drawn in as if he had lost his teeth, but there was the same handsome man, eyes turned slightly downward at their extremities, blond hair, strong jaw, an expression that said he was ready for an adventure or a laugh but always somehow ineffably sad. I stared at the lures and the photo for a long time. The lures were striper plugs with treble hooks and painted eyes of the sort that are used up and down the Jersey shore.

I had learned to fish from Johnny. We had begun with hand lines, not fishing rods. We had wound and unwound our fishing lines around sticks and cast the lines by swinging them overhead and throwing them over the water. We fished with a hook and sinker and night crawlers, and our catch was typically catfish or perch. Fishing with Johnny was always wrapped in some adventure. First we would have to start whatever broken-down car he happened to be driving, and this might involve pushing it down the street and hopping in and popping the clutch. Then would come the search for some secret spot that might require traversing an active railroad trestle with the tides rushing below, or renting a wooden boat and rowing into the current and dropping a concrete-block anchor to hold us steady as industrial barges passed by. The lures not only brought John back to me in a way, but they had the added poignancy of bringing him back to me as a boy and a young man. He was not only younger than I when he had used these fishing lures; he was younger than my son. They were artifacts of his life before he had come into ours, my mother's, Paul's and mine. I was surprised to learn that the lures even existed. I had never known him to own very much—a secondhand car, a good seaman's knife that he brought along on his merchant marine trips, a watch with a metal band, some changes of work clothes, and one good suit and a pair of polished black shoes. That was about it. It seemed that his entire life always had been able to fit in a seabag. The few things that he had given me—my first shotgun, a brass double-edge safety razor that operated by turning the handle to open the place where the blade was placed, those hand lines for fishing—had been lost through the years. Nothing more. So for me—who had brought no possessions from childhood into my adult life and had nothing to remember Johnny by except a few photographs—these lures instantly were prized possessions. I planned to clean the rust from the hooks and hang them in the cabin.

And then, almost at the same time, as if some sort of cosmic mechanism had been set in motion, I got a note from Johnny's niece, who, as it happened, was living in Maine. Would Paul and I like to have lunch with her and her mother? She had been a child of maybe four or five at the time that I was growing up in Silverton and living my life as a fisherman and trapper. Her father had been John's brother, and her family had lived not far from us. Her mother had been a close witness of my mother and John's marriage, and she had continued to see John after he'd disappeared from our lives. Chapters that I thought had closed for good were opening.

Over lunch, Paul and I asked a few questions and sat quietly and listened to the story of the final twenty years of John's life—the years of his life after he had left us. He had lived at first with his brother Charles not far from where we were living—so while his whereabouts were a mystery to us then, he had been only about ten miles away. Then he began drifting—he went to Florida, worked construction off and on, got involved there with a woman, whom he eventually would bring back to New Jersey, and shipped out again as a merchant seaman. All the time, his drinking worsened. He eventually found his way to New Orleans, where he lived for a number of years—maybe because there was a merchant marine union hall there—but then he returned to New Jersey. He was always the same John, she said, except that each year of drinking took a deeper toll on his health and appearance.

In the year before he died, she told us, he had been making a plan with his brother to visit my mother, Paul and me in Maine. It was going to be some sort of grand reunion. He was outfitting a van, she said, for the trip. (This had the ring of truth in it for me. He could not simply drive up; it was only an eight-hour trip with traffic, but he'd need to make it an adventure.)

"He loved you boys," she said.

By then, his hair was long and his cheeks were sunken between his jaws. His teeth were gone. In the last year of his life, his health had seriously deteriorated, and he was living at his mother's house in Spotswood and rarely came out of the bedroom where he slept. He was depressed and marking time until his death. It came as heart failure. His mother arranged for his burial at sea by the navy. There was no funeral.

Paul and I left the lunch stunned, trying to absorb these details.

Then, a few weeks later, came another bombshell. Paul told me that he and his wife had separated. The knot in the rope that I had sensed tightening inside of him through the previous year had suddenly come undone—and the rope went slack. He seemed relieved. I asked him if he needed to talk about it. "Not really," he said. "We'll see what happens." He took a long ride on his bike, and I saw him again the week before the holiday. He seemed okay. I guessed that he had already worked through the worst of the pain and disappointment of the break. Maybe this was the change I had witnessed over the summer.

Thanksgiving that year fell on November 26. By the weekend before that Thursday, it was clear that we would be close to completing the cabin but not fully done by the holiday. Paul's children had their hopes set on dinner at the cabin, and really so did Paul and I. We decided it would be our new family tradition. The cabin had heat, from Russell's woodstove, and water for the sink and toilet, and even gas for the lamps on the walls. The one missing item—so small yet so consequential—was a regulator, a fist-sized device necessary to connect the gas cooking stove to the pipe that brought the propane into the cabin from the storage tank outdoors. No regulator meant we had no stove, and no way to cook the turkey.

Paul had a solution. He bought a big turkey and stuffed it at home. (His stuffing was a sumptuous mix of bread, celery, sweet and hot Italian sausage and chunks of apple.) I rented a room at the inn the night before the meal, and he cooked the turkey in the oven of the kitchenette. The bird barely fit inside it. He also made gravy, mashed potatoes, lasagna, French-style string beans (with bacon and vinaigrette dressing), sweet potato casserole and cranberry relish. I brought Italian pastries from a bakery in Boston's North End and apple and pumpkin pies from Melby's. The kids came up in the afternoon—there was Paulie and Kevin; Katherine, her boyfriend and their two children; and Jodie and her boyfriend. I brought a friend from the university, a visiting scholar from Greece. He came with two bottles of wine from Crete. "So this is an American Thanksgiving?" he said, surveying the table and the rough interior of the cabin. The kids made a punch of raspberry ginger ale and sherbet. Paul had also brought a folding table and chairs from the church. We used a paper tablecloth and set the table with paper plates and plastic forks and knives. We built a fire in the woodstove and lit the gas lamps for light and a little extra heat.

"I'm hungry!" shouted Paulie.

"Everybody sit down," Paul hollered in a fake gruff voice.

We gathered around the table, and I said grace. I offered thanks for the food, for the presence of all of us together. I acknowledged the absence of my mother as I did each Thanksgiving. I said thanks for the cabin in which we were sheltered and for the plants and animals in the forest and for the gift of a year with my brother.

Paulie, squirming in his chair, spoke up. "Okay, okay. I'll say Amen to all that. And now let's eat!"

DREAMING OF APPLES

The winter following our first Thanksgiving in the cabin brought plenty of snow, but spring eventually made its welcome appearance, and I was there to greet it, pacing off an apple orchard. I liked the spot that I had been considering throughout the cabin's construction. I asked a state orchardist to have a look, and she thought its position on the slope was good.

Paul, Andrew and I cleared about half an acre for the orchard in March, about fifty yards above the cabin. We took down the oaks, maples and red pines that were there and bucked them into stove-sized sticks, which we heaped into four big piles of firewood. Then we laid out five lines for five rows of trees. I rented the auger machine that I had originally wanted to use for the foundation, and Paul and I dug fifty holes. If we hit a rock, we moved the machine a couple of inches to the right or left. Paul was less conscientious about the placement of the trees than he had been about the foundation piers. Maybe he was mellowing. The day was warm and the black flies made an early and fierce appearance, but we persisted and finished the job. We rewarded ourselves with a day of fishing in Great Brook. We caught a half dozen small trout and released them back into the stream. We napped in the sun and fished upstream toward the mountains with dry flies and napped some more. We pronounced it a successful day.

I ordered Macouns and McIntosh as my first apple varieties. They are good for eating, cooking and pressing for cider. The tiny trees, four-foot whips actually, came in early May from a nursery in Pennsylvania. They arrived in a cardboard box at the inn. Paul and I planted and watered them, and they have since thrived and put out new leaves and shoots. There was the one incident involving a hungry moose who took a liking to the green tips of the young trees on his way down to the pond, but he has since found his meals elsewhere and the trees have recovered. I'm pricing out a fence. I'm dreaming of that day when we put the ladders against the trees and fill baskets and barrels with apples. I will send them to friends, bake apple pies, sell them at the roadside and fill jugs of cider for distribution to my neighbors. Maybe I will learn to make applejack.

A cabin is an unending source of pleasant labor. I put down a little grass around its perimeter, which needs to be mowed every couple of weeks. There's painting indoors that remains undone, and I would like to build a bookcase in the bedroom. The barn is still a pile of beams stacked near the cabin's porch. I think I will carry it around in my head for another season or two to extract all the pleasure of anticipation before I turn it into the reality of work. I'm also thinking I could use a small sauna, and I'm wondering what it takes to build a cider press. I also have in mind a set of raised beds for a vegetable garden, and I would like to have a patch of raspberry vines. I've begun reading about the varieties.

They bear fruit from summer to fall, and some, especially the yellow varieties, bear fruit continuously from June through September. I have a good sunny spot in mind for them. I have also been reading about honeybees. I like honey in my tea, and all those bees would help with pollination in the orchard and raspberry patch.

Then there's the cabin's furniture. I'm adding to it slowly, from junk shops and the classifieds. I found a leather chair and ottoman for $150, which I dickered down to $125 and picked up at a swank condo on the Boston waterfront. It is a dark chocolate color and the ottoman is reddish brown. They make a handsome combination. My big find was a leather sofa. I had wanted a leather sofa for the cabin from the start—something comfortable and rugged and long enough to stretch out on for a night's sleep. I found one at a good price ($400) but it was on the third floor of a row house in Boston's North End, a famously dense neighborhood of narrow streets. It was too big to come down the stairs; it required a window exit from the third floor. I showed up with four long ropes and straps that tightened on ratchet wheels. The owner and I lashed two ropes around the sofa and took a turn around a beam inside the row house; then I lashed a third line to one end of the sofa and stationed a boy on the street to pull it away from the building as it came down to the sidewalk. A crowd gathered. The sofa descended slowly with all of us handling our ropes. There were no broken windows, rope burns or torn leather. I also found an inexpensive brass bed, and Paul donated a mattress and bedding.

As for the boys, Kevin is back to work. It's a job with a company that cleans and refurbishes boilers in generating plants. The work is hard but he makes good money. He's often on the road. Paulie is helping Andrew in his thriving boat engine repair business as he looks for a job as a motorcycle mechanic. Paul is now divorced, and he's still putting up commercial buildings in and around Portland. As I write this, he and I are planning a week at the cabin in November. We will have the boys and others who helped us along the way up for the opening of the deer season. Paul will be the cook and I will be the documentarian, and if nobody shoots a deer that will be fine too. It will carry on a long family tradition. I feel good about all of this. Later in the month, I will visit Adam and together we will try to get in some fishing. It will be spring in Peru. And there's this: a hawk has been visiting the hillside. He lands in a tree near the cabin and sits menacingly on a branch looking for quarry among the creases and folds of my hillside. I pay him no mind. He is casting no shadow.

ACKNOWLEDGMENTS

Among the books and articles that I consulted to write this book were William Hubbard's *A Narrative of the Troubles with the Indians in New England from Pascataqua to Pemmaquid*, which is the source for the story of the drowning of Squando's child; *The History of the Indian Wars in New England*, by William Hubbard, edited by S. G. Drake; *Dawnland Encounters: Indians and Europeans in Northern New England*, by Colin Calloway; the eminently readable *The Eastern Frontier: The Settlement of Northern New England, 1610–1763*, by Charles Clark, my former history teacher at the University of New Hampshire; *Lovewell's Town*, by Robert C. Williams, a town history written with the scholarship and sweep of a professional historian; *Blueberries and Pusley Weed*, by Pauline W. Moore, which provided marvelous detail on the early trades such as barrel making in the region; "The Rise and Decline of the Sheep Industry in North New England," by Harold Wilson; *The Name of War: King Philip's War and the Origins of American Identity*, by Jill Lepore; "King Philip's Herds: Indians, Colonists, and the Problem of Livestock in Early New England," by Virginia DeJohn Anderson; *The Path: A One-Mile Walk Through the Universe*, by Chet Raymo, a fascinating telling of the industrial and natural history of a New England town; *Reading the Forested Landscape: A Natural History of New England*, by Tom Wessels, an engaging guide to seeing the ways in which the history of middle New England is written on the wooded landscape; *The Northeast's Changing Forest* by Lloyd Irland, who has been researching and writing with intelligence and care about Maine's woodlands for decades; *Glaciers and Granite: A Guide to Maine's Landscape and Geology*, by David L. Kendall; *The Interrupted Forest: A History of Maine's Woodlands*, by Neil Rolde; and the unpublished journal of Sumner Kimball, a nineteenth-century Lovell farmer, which was made available to me by the Lovell Historical Society.

I also have many people to thank: Jill Kneerim, my agent, who has been a source of unflagging encouragement and guidance; Paul Slovak, my editor, for his early enthusiasm for the idea behind the book, his careful reading of the manuscript and his thoughtful suggestions; Trish Hall, of *The New York Times*, who embraced, shepherded and edited "From the Ground Up," the blog that I wrote for the *Times* as the cabin went up; the people of Stoneham, Maine, and especially Dan Barker, for his willingness to generously share his extensive knowledge of the town's past; the helpful staff at the Charlotte Hobbs Memorial Library in Lovell, where I often went to write in the summer of 2010; the librarians at the Maine Historical Society, who were always helpful; Laurie LaBar, chief curator of history and decorative arts at the Maine State Museum, who pointed me toward the military records of the Adams brothers; the Bethel Historical Society, for access to its archives, including old census data; the library staff of the National Museum of the American Indian in New York City; my graduate-student research assistants Emma Dong and Tina Tam; Boston University for supporting my work as a teacher and writer; and especially Sara Rimer. As my partner, she encouraged me to make myself into a writer. Without her, there would be no book. I also want to thank my daughter Elizabeth and my colleague Rob Manoff for their readings of the manuscript; my colleagues Mitch Zuckoff, Isabel Wilkerson, Nick Mills, Bob Zelnick and Richard Lehr for their encouragement and support; my nephews, Andrew, Kevin and Paulie for their hard work and good company along the way; and of course Paul, without whom there would be no cabin.

Also this: Just as no American can write a book about white whales without mentioning Melville and *Moby-Dick,* so no writer on the subject of cabins can fail to mention Henry Thoreau's masterpiece, *Walden.* I first read the book in high school, and while he and I went to the woods for different reasons and at different ages, and I make no pretense of trying to measure my modest effort against the greatness of his book, these acknowledgments would be incomplete without a deep bow to *Walden,* which, along with Thoreau's other writings, has had a profound effect on how I think about the world and the way to live in it.